Common Core Vocabulary Workbook Grades 4-7

JIREH PUBLISHERS

Common Core Vocabulary Workbook Grades 4-7

ID Simpson

About This Book

Designed for students in grades 4-7, the Common Core Vocabulary Workbook emphasizes essential vocabulary skills while laying a solid foundation for advanced vocabulary studies. By focusing on basic grammar rules and reading comprehension skills, this book offers a comprehensive approach to expanding and enhancing vocabulary skills. This book covers:

** prefixes
** suffixes
** analogies
** synonyms
** antonyms
** figurative language
** homonyms
** context clues
** compound words
** connotations
** denotations
** and more!

The Common Core Vocabulary Workbook, which meets Common Core Standards, is an invaluable companion for students aiming to build up and reinforce their vocabulary skills.

Table of Contents

Extending Vocabulary

Many English words come from the Latin and Greek languages. These words and word parts are called roots. Roots contain the basic meaning of a word and help you to define an unknown word. Prefixes and Suffixes may be added to a root word.

The base part of a word that a suffix or prefix is added to is called a root word. Root words contain the basic meaning of a word.

An affix is a letter or group of letters added to the beginning or end of a word. An affix added to the beginning of a word to change its meaning is called a prefix. An affix added to the end of a word to change its meaning is called a suffix. Suppose you had this question on a test:

Jean needed some material that would last for a long time. She purchased polyester because she believed it would be ________.

☐ deft ☐ delicate ☐ durable ☐ dainty

From reading the sentence, you know that Jean needs material that will last a long time. You know that dura is a root that means hard or lasting. Using the process of elimination, you know that the correct answer would be durable.

Many of our English prefixes come from the Latin and Greek languages. Some examples of Greek and Latin influences are in the example boxes below.

Prefixes / Roots	Meaning	Example
anti	against	anticrime
micro	small	microscope
pro	before	proactive
biblio, bibl	book	bibliography
geo	earth	geography
hydr	water	hydrate
therm	heat	thermometer
homo	same	homophone
mono	one	monopoly
extra	beyond	extraordinary
phon	sound	telephone
chron	time	chronological
psych	mind	psychology
cosmo	universe	cosmology
bio	life	biography
auto	self	autobiography
aster, astro	star	asteroid, astrology

Prefixes / Roots	Meaning	Example
pre	before	preexist
aqua	water	aquarium
act	do	action
audi	to hear	audible
port	carry	portable
bene	well or good	beneficial
temp	time	temporary
dict	say, speak	dictate
re	back, again	repeat
sub	under	submarine
cent	one hundred	centimeter
cur	run, happen	current
semi	half, two	semicircle
circum	around	circumvent
ante	before	antebellum
ad	to, toward	adverb
inter	between	interconnected
post	after	postgame
quad	four	quadrilateral
deci	ten	decimal
tri	three	trifold
pent	five	pentagon
bi	two	bicycle

Using Roots and Affixes to Expand Vocabulary

Directions: You can add beginnings (prefixes) and endings (suffixes) to root words. When you combine root words with prefixes or suffixes, new words are created. Knowing about root words, suffixes, and prefixes can help you determine the meaning of unfamiliar words.

Examples

1.	**Prefix**	**Root**	**Suffix**	**New Word**
	dis	embark		disembark
2.		embarrass	ed	embarrassed
3.	pre	dawn		predawn
4.		obtain	able	obtainable
5.	bi	lingual		bilingual
6.	re	play	ed	replayed
7.	un	comfort	able	uncomfortable
8.	im	port		import
9.	in	tolerant		intolerant
10.	un	obtain	able	unobtainable
11.	con	struct		construct
12.		frag	ment	fragment
13.	pro	claim		proclaim
14.	mal	function	ing	malfunctioning
15.		wet	ness	wetness
16.	un	known		unknown

Directions: Knowing the root or affix of a word can help you narrow down the meaning. After reading the root and its meaning, select the best answer.

Root	Meaning
fract, frag	break
mega	big

1. To fracture a leg is to ____________ it.

☐ hit it hard ☐ get a big bruise ☐ crack

Root	Meaning
dem	people
cratic	government

2. A democratic government is one that ________________________.

☐ is ran by one person ☐ represents the people ☐ changes each year

Root	Meaning
migra	wander
cur	happen

3. The ____________ of people caused the town to be nearly empty.

☐ current ☐ migration ☐ estimation

Root	Meaning
hydr	water
de	down, off, away
hyper	above normal

4. He was so _____________ from the lack of water that he nearly fainted.

☐ hydrated ☐ hyperlinked ☐ dehydrated

Root	Meaning
proto	first
post	after

5. Even though the model had been updated many times, I still preferred the original _________.

☐ prototype ☐ protagonist ☐ postgame

Root	Meaning
terra	earth
extra	beyond, outside
uni	one

6. Some people believe there is ______________ life in space.

☐ terrain ☐ territorial ☐ extraterrestrial

Root	Meaning
geo	earth
graph	written or drawn
metry	process of measuring

7. ________________ is the study of the earth.

☐ Geometry ☐ Geography ☐ Geometric

Root	Meaning
bene	good, well

8. A benevolent person is one _____________________________________.

☐ who gives only if he gets something in return ☐ who gives freely and generously
☐ who gives only if someone is looking

Root	Meaning
mal	bad, badly

9. A person who is maladjusted is one who is______________________________.

☐ well adjusted ☐ poorly adjusted ☐ perfect

Root	Meaning
hex	six

10. A hexagon has _______ sides.

☐ 10 ☐ 6 ☐ 4

Root	Meaning
contra	against
pro	for

11. To contradict someone, you speak ________________.

☐ in support of him ☐ against him ☐ but don't make a final decision

Root	Meaning
derm	skin
opto	optic, vision
dent	tooth

12. A ______________________ is a doctor who cares for your skin.

☐ optometrist ☐ dermatologist ☐ dentist

Root	Meaning
gastr	stomach
ped, pod	foot

13. A gastric disorder is a disorder in the ____________________.

☐ brain ☐ feet ☐ stomach

Root	Meaning
magni	great, big
mini	small

14. To magnify means to make __________.

☐ tiny ☐ bigger ☐ zilch

Root	Meaning
hyper	over
hypo	under

15. If you have hypertension, you have _________ blood pressure. If you have hypotension, you have ______________ blood pressure.

☐ low, high ☐ high, medium ☐ high, low

Root	Meaning
spect	to look
co	with, together
anti	against

16. He decided to be a _______________ that cheered for the team.

☐ antihero ☐ cooperator ☐ spectator

Root	Meaning
sub	below
trans	on to the other side
re	back, from

17. The ship _____________ us back to the pier.

☐ submerged ☐ reverted ☐ transported

Root	Meaning
audi	hear

18. The _____________ clapped for several minutes.

☐ audition ☐ audience ☐ auditorium

Root	Meaning
dict	say, speak

19. She _____________ that her team would win the game.

☐ contradict ☐ dictated ☐ predicted

Prefixes

Prefixes are added to the front of roots. When you add a prefix, it often changes the meaning of a word.

Examples: in + bound = inbound = coming in
dis + unity = disunity = not united
mis + step = misstep = incorrect step

Directions: Have the students write a minimum of four words using the prefixes anti, re, dis, non, and pre. Have them write the definition of each word.

Possible Answers

Prefix anti: The meaning is against.

1. antisocial: against established social order

2. antipollution: against pollution

3. antidote: used as a remedy against poison

4. hero: not having heroic qualities

Prefix re: The meaning is back or again.

1. replay: play something again

2. reassure: restore to confidence

3. recoil: shrink back

4. recondition: restore to good condition

Prefix dis: The meaning is not; opposite of

1. disagree: have a differing opinion

2. displeased: not pleased; dissatisfied

3. disarm: not armed; to deprive of the means of attack or defense

4. discomfort: not comfortable; mental or bodily distress

Prefix non: the meaning is not.

1. nonconformist: not conforming; one who refuses to be bound by accepted beliefs, customs, or practices

2. nonbeliever: not a believer

3. nonfiction: not fiction; work other than fiction

4. nonessential: not necessary; having little or no importance

Prefix pre: The meaning is earlier; before.

1. predict: tell something before it happens

2. prepare: get ready beforehand

3. precede: come before

4. preamble: an introductory statement

Prefixes

Directions: Complete each word using a prefix from the word bank.

auto	pre	mis
in	dis	re
sub	non	
mid	bi	
post	im	

1. _____pact

2. _____significant

3. _____noculars

4. _____biography

5. _____sense

6. _____season

7. _____merge

8. _____capable

9. _____interpret

10. _____believed

11. _____night

12. _____ply

13. _____dict

14. Which one of the following is not a prefix?

☐ ness ☐ un ☐ mis ☐ dis

15. Which of the following are prefixes?

☐ est ☐ fore ☐ trans ☐ non

Prefixes

Directions: Complete each word using a prefix from the word bank. Some prefixes may be used more than once.

Prefix	Definition
re	back, again
tri	three
temp	time
auto	self
anti	against
chron	time
bene	good
therm	heat
pro	for, in support of
circum	around
semi	half, partially
hydr	water
aqua	water
micro	small
quad	four

1. __________ogen
2. __________scope
3. __________matic
4. __________ometer
5. __________stance
6. __________ficial
7. __________peller
8. __________monthly
9. __________cipate
10. __________angle
11. __________orary
12. __________ological
13. __________rilateral
14. __________ tic
15. __________direct

Prefixes

Directions: Identify the meaning of the underlined words by using the provided prefixes and context clues.

Prefix	Meaning
amphi	both

1. Amphibians can live on ________________
- ☐ land only
- ☐ water, land, and air
- ☐ land and water

Prefix	Meaning
bi	two

2. You receive a paycheck biweekly. How often are you paid?
- ☐ once a month
- ☐ every two weeks
- ☐ every two days

Prefix	Meaning
hemi, semi	half

3. A semicircle is what percentage of a circle?
- ☐ 75 %
- ☐ 90%
- ☐ 50%

Prefix	Meaning
micro	small

4. Even though a microbe is ___________, it can produce disease.
- ☐ broad
- ☐ tiny
- ☐ big

Prefix	Meaning
astro	star

5. Lee loves astronomy because he believes in extraterrestrials. Lee loves to ________.

☐ study cooking starchy foods
☐ watch movies
☐ study space

Prefix	Meaning
tri	three

6. Trixie loves to ride on her tricycle. It has __________ wheels.

☐ four
☐ three
☐ two

Prefix	Meaning
oct	eight

7. An octopus has ____________ legs.

☐ six
☐ two
☐ eight

Prefix	Meaning
auto	self

8. When a person writes an autobiography, he is writing about ______________.

☐ family and friends
☐ a fictional character
☐ himself

Prefix	Meaning
post	after
pre	before

9. She arrived at the hospital at 8:00 a.m. for preoperative testing. At 12:00 p.m. she was moved to a postoperative room. The 8:00 a.m. testing was ___________ her surgery. She was moved to the postoperative room ___________ the surgery.

☐ before; for
☐ after; immediately before
☐ before; after

Prefix	Meaning
quad	four

10. Quadruple eight. What number do you get?
☐ 32
☐ 54
☐ 48

Prefix	Meaning
cent	hundred

11. How many years are in a century?
☐ 500
☐ 250
☐ 100

Prefix	Meaning
circum	around

12. The kids ran the circumference of the yard. They ran ____________ the yard.
☐ halfway through
☐ completely around
☐ straight through

Prefix	Meaning
macro	large

13. If a company is doing a macroanalysis on why people prefer certain name brands, it is doing a study ____________________________.
☐ small in scope
☐ hefty in scope
☐ diminutive in scope

Prefix	Meaning
sub	under

14. A ship moves ____________ the water. A submarine moves __________ the water.
☐ under, on top of
☐ on top of, under
☐ on top of, on top

Suffixes

A suffix is one or more-word parts added to the end of a root word. A suffix cannot stand alone.

Suppose you had this question on a test:

Earth's natural resources aren't __________________. If we waste them, we will lose them. For that reason, we need to use them wisely, reuse them when possible, and recycle.

☐ abhorrent ☐ vulnerable ☐ sustainable ☐ scarce

Sustain is a root word that means continue or support. Able is a suffix that means capacity to do. Using the process of elimination, you could deduce that the correct answer would be sustainable.

Many of our English suffixes come from the Latin and Greek languages. Some examples of Greek and Latin influences are in the example boxes below.

Suffixes / Roots	Meanings	Examples
meter	to measure	speedometer
cracy	power, rule	democracy
logy	study of	biology
scope	look at, see	microscope
nym	name	homonym
oid	resembling	meteoroid
ist	one who practices, skilled	journalist
ergy	work, effect	allergy
graph	write, draw	photograph
log	word, speak	backlog
able	capacity to do	sustainable
naut	voyager	astronaut
pod	foot	tripod
phone	sound	speakerphone
ful	full of	mouthful
ion	act, process, condition	possession
ate	to cause, acted upon	passionate
mit	send	admit
ly	like, in the manner of	quickly
ed	makes a verb past tense	waited
s	makes a word plural	ducks
es	makes a word plural	buses
vert	turn	convert

Suffixes / Roots	Meanings	Examples
est	comparative (most)	smallest
er	comparative (more)	larger
port	carry	seaport
ous	full of, quality of	perilous
tract	drag, pull	subtract
less	lacking, without	fearless
ing	makes a verb past tense	sailing
ish	in the manner of, like	childish
some	group of, quality of	foursome
ward	certain direction	forward
ible	ability, capable of	terrible
ance	action, state, quality	performance
ship	position held, quality, state	hardship
ery	condition, behavior, place	machinery
ness	quality, state, action	kindness
sion	state, action, condition	confusion
al	result of, pertaining to	arrival
ive	a state of	active
ity	a state of	brevity
age	act, process, condition	acreage
ize	make, cause to become	capitalize
ility	ability	responsibility
ment	act, process of	achievement
y	being like	grouchy
like	similar to	childlike
ous	full of	humorous
fold	many parts	tenfold

Suffixes

Directions: Make a new word by combining the word and suffix. You may have to add or drop some letters. Look at the example below.

Word +	Suffix =	Word
account +	able =	accountable
recognize +	tion =	recognition
argue +	ment =	argument
beauty +	ful =	beautiful

1. danger + ous =

2. fame + ous =

3. fashion + able =

4. usual + ly =

5. mountain + ous =

6. practical + ly =

7. pity + ous =

8. accident + ally =

9. favor + able =

10. admission + ible =

11. logical + ly =

12. marvel + ous =

13. assess + ment =

14. abnormal + ly =

15. beautiful + ly =

16. allege + ation =

17. dispose + al =

18. create + ive =

19. happy + ily =

20. peril + ous =

Suffixes

Directions: Add the correct suffix to the underlined word in each sentence.

1. She was very care___ in doing her work. She was in a hurry to go outside.

☐ ful ☐ less ☐ log

2. Whenever he didn't get his way, he would act very child___ .

☐ ful ☐ ish ☐ less

3. Even though everyone else looked glum, Dan was cheer___.

☐ ful ☐ less ☐ tract

4. I didn't believe her story. She just didn't seem truth___ .

☐ meter ☐ able ☐ ful

5. This is the bigg___ piece of cake I have ever had.

☐ ness ☐ er ☐ est

6. Since she was new, she was not comfort______ in the school.

☐ less ☐ able ☐ er

7. The party was really awe____ .

☐ some ☐ ion ☐ fy

8. He was a natural art___.

☐ ist ☐ est ☐ ly

9. Since she showed great responsib____, Tonya was allowed to stay home by herself.

☐ some ☐ ous ☐ ility

10. His song about love is considered to be beauti___.

☐ logy ☐ ful ☐ ion

11. I am ten feet from the door. Since my teacher is five feet away, she is clos____ to the door.

☐ er ☐ ful ☐ ous

12. It took Liz so long to achieve her dream that even she wondered if it would material

☐ ly ☐ ness ☐ ize

13. Be care___ when solving your math problems.

☐ less ☐ ble ☐ ful

14. I love animals so much that I want to study zoo____.

☐ ist ☐ logy ☐ ful

15. If you keep picking at your sore, you will get an infect__ .

☐ able ☐ ion ☐ ize

16. Since Jean has asthma, she needs an inhal__ to help her breathe.

☐ er ☐ ed ☐ cracy

17. She felt feverish, so she checked her temperature with a thermo______.

☐ vert ☐ ergy ☐ meter

18. He wanted to take act____, rather than to sit around and wait.

☐ ous ☐ less ☐ ion

Suffixes

Directions: Use a suffix from the word bank below to make a word.

al	graph	er
ize	less	ous
ship	able	ergy
ate	ment	y
ly	ful	ness

1. meaning__________
2. acknowledge__________
3. train__________
4. danger__________
5. salt__________
6. approach__________
7. real__________
8. venge__________
9. comic__________
10. auto__________
11. decor__________
12. all__________
13. sad__________
14. dutiful__________
15. space__________

Suffixes

Directions: Use a suffix from the word bank below to make a word.

ist	ence	cy
ward	hood	ty
ier	wise	dom
ary	some	ish
ian	an	tic

1. after__________

2. slug__________

3. pover__________

4. antibio__________

5. bore__________

6. conspira__________

7.magic__________

8. consequ__________

9. adult__________

10. spokeswom__________

11. awe__________

12. counterclock__________

13. front__________

14.sedent__________

15. tour__________

Prefixes and Suffixes

Directions: Add a prefix and/or suffix to each word from the word bank to make two new words. The first one is done for you. Note: Some prefixes and suffixes may be used more than once.

ment	ly	re	un	al
ed	ion	able	ian	y
ing	ary	in	mis	ably
iest	ity			

swirl	**swirled**	**swirling**
popular		
assure		
fashion		
cap		
recognize		
relent		
possess		
flinch		
imagine		
music		
educate		
usual		
control		
invent		
visible		
embellish		
thrift		
enchant		

Prefixes and Suffixes

Directions: Underline the prefix and/or suffix in each word.

1. designer
2. misspell
3. humorist
4. import
5. kilogram
6. amusement
7. antifreeze
8. postgraduate
9. microscope
10. reverse
11. capable
12. extractor
13. preamble
14. freedom
15. duckling
16. photograph
17. reheat
18. questionable
19. triangle
20. nonfat
21. intake
22. zoology
23. empower
24. lessee
25. internalize
26. uniform

Prefixes and Suffixes

Directions: Read each paragraph below. Fill in the blank with the correct word.

1. Billy hit another ____________________ while driving too fast. Instead of waiting for the ____________________ to take him to the hospital, he slowly ____________________ out of his car. He found out later that if his car would have been a manual transmission instead of an ____________________, he probably would have died.

ambulance automatic automobile ambled

2. After not seeing her all day, Jean was wondering why Sue had been ____________________ from school. Sue did not have many friends because she was very quiet and ____________________. Due to her ____________________behavior, no one besides Sue wondered if Jean was ____________________.

absent unwell introverted antisocial

3. It's no fun being ____________________ from school functions. I don't know why my friends won't ____________________ me. It seems as if they only do things to ____________________themselves. Nothing that they ever do is ____________________ to me.

beneficial include benefit excluded

4. She lies so much that she is known as an ____________________ person. She is simply ____________________. She ____________________ forgets what she tells us. She said that she went to Dan's party, although she initially told us that she was sick the night of the party. She often ____________________ herself.

contradicts incredible untruthful constantly

5. We sprayed air freshener to ____________________ the room. The smell was so ____________________ that we had to open all the windows. The ____________________ of the room gradually lessened the ____________________ odor.

unpleasant ventilation disagreeable deodorize

6. Our first group project was ____________________ because of ____________________. Our teacher attributed it to constant ____________________. He said the project was a ____________________ mess instead of a unified effort.

disjointed disorganization infighting rejected

7. She ____________________ the directions I gave her. Even though it was her mistake, somehow, she felt that I had ____________________ her. Despite her belief, I refuse to completely ____________________ her grade. She can ____________________ the paper for extra credit if she wants a better grade.

misinformed reconsider misinterpreted rewrite

8. The children sat in a ____________________ waiting for the ____________________ game to start. The children believed the star player to be an ____________________ athlete. The excitement of waiting for him to come on the field and play was ____________________.

semifinal unbearable semicircle extraordinary

9. The ____________________ arrived to help the man stuck in his ____________________. They knew that to be ____________________ in helping the man, they had to ____________________ with caution.

successful paramedics proceed parachute

10. Even though she knew her child was ____________________ and ____________________, James and Charity were ____________________ to criticism. They finally accepted that something needed to be done after their family staged an ____________________.

undisciplined hypersensitive intervention hyperactive

11. In ____________________, she wished she had done things differently. She faced a ____________________ of problems, and they seemed to be ____________________ daily. Honestly looking back, she realized that it was entirely her fault.

multitude honestly retrospect multiplying

12. Reggie decided that he would not allow Eric, his boss, to ____________________ him anymore. An ____________________ man, Eric would ____________________ take advantage of Reggie's meek temperament. Although he claimed to ____________________ step on Reggie's toes every day, Reggie believed Eric's actions were intentional.

disrespect constantly accidentally inconsiderate

Analogy

An analogy is a comparison between two things. Some different types of analogies are:

1. Characteristic - compares features
2. Antonym - compares words that have opposite meanings
3. Synonym - compares words that have similar meanings
4. Part/Whole - compares part of a particular thing to the whole thing
5. Classification - compares class or grouping
6. Function - what a particular thing does to the thing that does it
7. Cause/Effect - compares the cause to the result/effect

Definitions of Symbols Used In Analogies

: means is to or are to

:: means as

Analogy	Examples
Characteristic	loyalty : true friend:: lawlessness : thief
	red : strawberry :: blue : blueberry
Antonym	friend : enemy :: love: hate
	positive image : negative image :: high self-esteem : low self-esteem
Synonym	mistake : error :: change : adjust
	regret : feel remorse :: happy : ecstatic
Part/Whole	finger : hand :: toe : foot
	books : library :: teachers : school
Classification	cat : pet :: jaguar : wild animal
	fiction : literature :: geometry : math
Function	artists : paint :: teachers : teach
	ruler : size :: compass : direction
Cause/Effect	extreme heat : drought :: excessive rain : flood
	medicine : heal :: fall: bruise

Analogies

Directions: Complete the analogies below.

1. zoologist : animals :: archaeologist : _______________

☐ plants ☐ fossils_ ☐ weather

2. amateur : expert :: supporter : _______________

☐ adversary ☐ friend ☐ well-wisher

3. site : sight :: here : _________

☐ hear ☐ hare ☐ hair

4. ewe : lamb :: kitten : _______________

☐ cat ☐ ox ☐ child

5. hexagon : 6 :: square : _______________

☐ 5 ☐ 4 ☐ 7

6. pig : piglet :: cow : _______________

☐ hatchling ☐ calf ☐ kit

7. sophisticated : elegant :: ugly : ____________

☐ beautiful ☐ hideous ☐ sparkly

8. before : prefix :: ending : ___________

☐ synonym ☐ antonym ☐ suffix

9. books : literature :: percentage : __________

☐ math ☐ social studies ☐ science

10. camels : desert :: foxes : ________________

☐ land and water ☐water ☐ forest

11. carnivores : meat eaters :: herbivores : ____________

☐ eats both plant and animals ☐ plant eaters ☐ meat eaters

12. pediatrician : child's health care :: optometrist : _______________

☐ eye health ☐ oral health ☐ exercise tips

13. treadmill : run :: water :________________

☐ drinking ☐ swim ☐ thirst

14. horses : herd :: geese : _____________

☐ swarm ☐ colony ☐ gaggle

15. artist : painting :: poet : __________________

☐ poetry ☐ books ☐ drawings

16. wings : airplane :: sentence : __________________

☐ library ☐ paragraph ☐ literature

17. error : mistake :: disheveled : __________________

☐ cars ☐ houses ☐ rumpled

Analogies

Directions: Choose a vocabulary word from the words below to complete each analogy. The first one is done for you. All words will not be used.

mammal	weight	emotion	beagle	pencil
brew	coop	conjunction	wheat	stereotype
prune	vegetable	audible	exception	opinion
pupil	book	mimic	characters	snobbish

1. spacious : large :: imitate : mimic

2. nonfiction : fiction :: fact :

3. lawn mower : grass :: scythe :

4. peculiar : odd :: standoffish :

5. water: fish :: land :

6. movie : actors :: story :

7. dinosaur : T-Rex :: dog :

8. verb : action :: interjection :

9. ink : pen :: lead :

10. August : noun :: or :

11. letter : thank you :: report :

12. bread : bake :: coffee :

13. mouth : tongue :: eyes :

14. lion : den :: chicken ::

15. knife : cut :: shears :

16. degree : temperature :: ounce :

Analogies

Directions: Choose a vocabulary word from the word bank below to complete each analogy. The first one is done for you. All words will not be used.

scratch	California	shop	chirp	accidents
textbooks	temperature	dairy	tool	gosling
corrosion	lay	biased	essential	tree
river	swam	10 years	twigs	loud
breeze	dutiful	tolerate	propose	notebook

1. woman : baby girl :: goose : gosling

2. scrap : abolish :: necessary :

3. century : 100 years :: decade :

4. dogs : bark :: birds :

5. library : quiet :: football game :

6. germs : disease :: carelessness :

7. tulip : flower :: oak :

8. lamp : light :: fan :

9. ruthless : brutal :: deterioration :

10. Richmond : Virginia :: Sacramento :

11. primary sources : letters :: secondary sources :

12. plants : seedling :: tree :

13. patience : impatience :: impartial :

14. beans : legumes :: milk :

15. choose : chose :: swim :

16. clock : time :: thermometer :

17. sleepy : yawn :: itch :

18. hill : mountain :: creek :

Synonyms

Directions: Synonyms are words that have similar meanings. For example, fall and stumble have similar meanings. Match each word to its synonym in the word bank. The first one is done for you.

Word Bank Box

influence	cushioned	option
agonized	sad	clarify
accentuated	emerge	frustrate
modern	noncompliant	swirl
overwhelming	defiant	antique
glow	perturbed	encased

1. old - antique

2. emphasized -

3. appear -

4. new -

5. insubordinate -

6. pained -

7. disappointed -

8. radiate -

9. unruly -

10. buffered -

11. upset -

12. impact -

13. overpowering -

14. revolve -

15. disappoint -

16. choice -

17. explain -

18. enclosed -

Synonyms

Directions: Synonyms – words that have similar meanings. Match each word to its synonym in the word bank. The first one is done for you.

unwell	bubbling	gigantic	cheerful	counterfeit
oppress	smuggled	consume	impressive	compensate
ignite	regenerate	firm	puzzled	blunder
flexible	outpouring	accomplished	worn	good - humored
bargain	wide	expel	rock	uninjured

1. fake - counterfeit

2. cheap -

3. persecute -

4. renew -

5. sway -

6. steady -

7. versatile -

8. amiable -

9. broad -

10. contraband -

11. haggard -

12. perky -

13. sick -

14. skilled -

15. unscathed -

16. kick out -

17. surge -

18. remunerate -

19. perplexed -

20. massive -

21. kindle -

22. ingest -

23. grandiose -

24. fumble -

25. frothy -

Antonyms

Antonyms are words that have opposite meanings. For example, take the word *dirty*. The opposite of *dirty* is *clean*.

Directions: Find the antonym for each word below by choosing a word from the text box below. The first one is done for you.

familiar	safe	unreasonable	deposit
smother	squalor	fatherly	nice
malnourished	ignorance	ignite	create
unrealistic	young	beautiful	strong
intentional	miserable	scarce	illuminated

1. knowledge - ignorance

2. destroy -

3. happy -

4. logical -

5. nasty-

6. withdraw -

7. ancient -

8. darkened -

9. feeble -

10. grotesque -

11. dangerous -

12. maternal -

13. neglect -

14. peculiar -

15. practical -

16. obese -

17. abundant -

18. luxury -

19. accidental -

20. extinguish -

Antonyms

Directions: Match each word to its antonym in the word bank.

infinite	dry	ill	artificial	joy
despise	angelic	detract	clumsy	sluggish
destroy	free	fumble	follow	blunder
answer	refrain	poisonous	miserly	excited
boorish	enormous	deafening	weathered	rigid

1. graceful -

2. swift -

3. polite -

4. lead -

5. fail -

6. engage -

7. pristine -

8. healthy -

9. catch -

10. edible -

11. miniature -

12. natural -

13. naughty -

14. moist -

15. question -

16. flexible -

17. enhance -

18. grief -

19. preserve -

20. restrained -

21. giving -

22. peaceful -

23. bore -

24. enjoy -

25. few -

Figurative Language

Figurative language is used for effect. For example, take the phrase dead tired. The phrase dead tired does not mean the person is dead. The word dead is used to emphasize the degree of tiredness. There are different types of figurative language. Below are the five types of figurative language.

1. Simile: a comparison of two different things that use the words like or as.

2. Metaphor: a comparison of two different things that does not use the words like or as.

3. Personification: the giving of human qualities to animals or objects.

4. Idiom: an expression that has a totally different meaning from its individual words.

5. Hyperbole: an exaggerated comparison.

Examples

1. The cake was calling my name. (personification)

2. It's raining cats and dogs. (idiom)

3. That stubborn mule, Candice, refused to consider that she was wrong. (metaphor)

4. After losing the big race, she and her teammates drowned their disappointments with a bottle of soda. (idiom)

5. Tall as Mount Everest, he was easily the largest kid in the class. (hyperbole and simile)

6. It was so resplendent that it reminded her of droplets of rain dancing on leaves in the sunlight. (personification)

7. The pie tasted like cardboard. (simile)

8. I have tried a million times. (hyperbole)

9. The teapot screamed at me when it was ready. (personification)

Idioms

We use idioms in our everyday speech. An idiom is an expression that has a meaning apart from the meaning of its individual words. An idiom should not be taken literally.

Examples: My little brother is a pain in the butt.

☐ is helpful to me
☐ had a pain in his butt
☐ was bothersome

My mom knows how to cook a cake from scratch.

☐ defrost a cake
☐ with a cake mix from the store
☐ from raw ingredients

1. Nikko did not allow Mr. Perkin's to throw a wet blanket on how he felt.

☐ to encourage him
☐ to discourage him
☐ to provoke him

2. Tiera was dog tired after working with her mom.

☐ unhappy
☐ excited
☐ exhausted

3. Excited to see her best friend perform on stage, he told her to break a leg.

☐ harm herself
☐ hurt someone else
☐ do well

4. Walter thought Annie was yellow - bellied because she didn't want to fight to be a cheerleader.

☐ a fighter
☐ a coward
☐ an instigator

5. Ms. Jenkins had been discouraged year in and year out by students not keeping their promises.

☐ constantly
☐ very seldom
☐ never

6. Wealthy and popular, Laurie felt that she didn't have to work for what she wanted because she was the cream of the crop.

☐ the best
☐ at the bottom of the pack
☐ occasionally winning

7. Betty was not Jason's cup of tea because of differing personalities.

☐ favorite flavor
☐ preference
☐ personal drinking cup

8. Reggie didn't want to talk and beat around the bush.

☐ pruned
☐ jumped in
☐ delay

9. With few better options, she bit the bullet.

☐ did it despite hesitation
☐ hesitated
☐ bit the bullet for iron

10. Even though Betty had screwed up academically, she was determined that she would make a change.

☐ done a great job
☐ messed up
☐ tightened her screws

Idioms

Directions: Read each idiom below. Choose the best word or phrase from the word box that is most similar in meaning. The first one is done for you. All words/phrases will not be used.

runs smoothly	encourage	bad attitude, grudge	maneuver	agree with
skip steps	unable to see well	canoe	angrily act in a way that will end a relationship	fearful person
quarter	listen carefully	consumption	take a risk	jealous
happy	only caring about himself/herself	anxious	raining hard	unkempt hair
misbehave	borrow money	snobbish	propose	person that agrees with everything

1. raining cats and dogs - raining hard
2. see eye to eye -
3. stuck up
4. green with envy -
5. chip on his shoulder -
6. yes man -
7. go like clockwork -
8. cut corners -
9. stick your neck out -
10. scaredy cat -
11. all ears -
12. egg on -
13. looking out for number one -
14. sunny disposition -
15. standing on pins and needles -
16. blind as a bat -
17. burn bridges -

Hyperbole

Hyperbole is a type of figurative language. It often compares two objects by exaggerating or overstating.

Examples: Mary's head is ten times bigger than the sun.

* Mary's head is being compared to the sun.

I have told you a million times to be quiet.

* It's impossible to tell someone something that many times.

Directions: Use the words and phrases in the word bank to complete each of the hyperbolic statements. The first one is done for you.

walked on it, it broke	around the world in one day	big as saucers	could hear him 250 miles away
you could see 5,000 miles away	cockroaches protested and left	her face lit up brighter than a light bulb	runs away from him
trillion times a day	couldn't fit any other information into it	could float on top	gain weight
she jumped clear across the room	came out of it when she opened it	my eardrums burst	

1. Just looking at food makes me gain weight.

2. The coffee was so thick that a cruise ship ____________________.

3. The cat's eyes were ____________________.

4. The window was so clean that ____________________.

5. He whistled so loud that ____________________.

6. Her purse was so big that a marching band ____________________.

7. You are on my mind at least a ____________________.

8. The chair was so fragile that when an ant ____________________.

9. I studied so hard that my brain ____________________.

10. He lies so much that the truth ____________________.

11. Her car is so fast that she could drive ____________________.

12. When my father found out that I failed class, he yelled so loud that my grandmother

____________________.

13. The house was so filthy that the ____.

14. When she found out that she won the contest, ______________________________.

15. After discovering the bug hanging above her, _______________________________.

Similes & Metaphors

Directions: Identify each sentence as a simile or metaphor. The first one is done for you.

Simile: a comparison that uses the words like or as.

Metaphor: a comparison that does not use the words like or as.

1. The food was like a drug. simile
2. She was cool as a cucumber.
3. She was sharp as a pin.
4. Her house is an icebox.
5. The sudden downpour came down in piercing needle.
6. The sun bursting through the clouds was a ray of hope that my dreams would come true.
7. She was like a wild animal running around untamed.
8. His cruel words were a bullet to my bruised heart.
9. The moon beams were like a guide dog showing us the way home.
10. The ice cream is as hard as a brick.
11. The baby was a bundle of joy.
12. Life is a journey full of pleasant sights and wrong turns.
13. His feet are as long as a submarine.
14. She is as tall as a skyscraper.
15. His eyes are the color of the ocean after a storm.
16. The water is as clear as newly cleaned glass.
17. The turkey was lean like a ballerina.
18. He is as cool as ice.
19. She sweats like a hog.
20. She is as clean as a whistle.

Alliterations

Alliteration is the repetition or use of the same consonant sound at the beginning of a phrase or sentence.

Example #1: <u>T</u>iny <u>T</u>im stood <u>t</u>all.

- The letter T is repeated at the beginning of more than two words in this sentence.

Example #2: <u>S</u>he was <u>s</u>afe and <u>s</u>ound.

- The letter S is repeated at the beginning of more than two words in this sentence.

Directions: Read each sentence/phrase below. Identify if the sentence has an alliteration and underline all the words with the same beginning sound. The first one is done for you.

1.The food was bountiful. <u>not an alliteration</u>

2. Abby ate an apple afterward.

3. Quentin quickly put the quill quietly away.

4. I went shopping downtown yesterday.

5. Goosy Goose

6. Sleepy and Sluggish

7. In the Jungle

8. Abby ate an apple.

9. Ticker Ticker Toc

10. Welcome Home

11. Moody Max

12. She had a sweet sixteen birthday party.

13. Sullen Susan stayed still.

14. She didn't care about what other people thought.

15. The radio is too loud.

16. I really don't care what you say.

Imagery

Imagery is the use of a vivid description to create pictures or images in the reader's mind.

Directions: Read the following poem and answer the following questions.

She stood out like a sore thumb,
In a dress the color of a plum.
Eyes wide with fright,
Yellow and orange streaks in hair dark as night.
All of that made her look a total sight.
Her mouth slightly open, curved to one side
Showing two oversized sharp fangs that seemed impossible to hide.
With two tiny feet, small as a snail,
A long giraffe neck and skin white and pale.
I watched her as she silently began to steal away
Being glad that it was the end of the day

Answer the following:

1. Identify the 2 similes in the poem.

2. Identify the 2 idioms in the poem.

3. Draw and color a picture of her in the space below.

Onomatopoeia Words

Onomatopoeia words describe the sounds that objects and people make. Look at the examples below.

Animal/Object/People	Sound
Cat	Meow
Ghost	Boo
Clock	Tick
Excited Person	Woo-Hoo

Directions: Read the poem below. Underline the onomatopoeia words. Reread the poem and make the sounds instead of saying the words.

Noise! Noise! Noise!
Everywhere I go
I always hear noise!
Water splashing.
Tires squealing.
Rain trickling.
Horns honking.
Pots banging.
Bees buzzing.
Frogs croaking.
But the best noise of all
Is the pitter patter feet
Of my baby boy Skeet.

Onomatopoeia Words

Directions: Look at each onomatopoeia word in the text box. Put each word in the correct category. Some words may fit in multiple categories.

whoosh	oink	sizzle	bang	bray	splash
neigh	crack	slam	honk	cluck	growl
drip	hoot	buzz	chirp	beep-beep	vroom
bellow	ring	roar	squeak	snap	croak
tick tock	trumpet	bleat	tweet	ding dong	twang

Sounds that Animals Make	Sounds of Inanimate Objects
1.	1.
2.	2.
3.	3.
4.	4.
5.	5.
6.	6.
7.	7.
8.	8.
9.	9.
10.	10.
11.	11.
12.	12.
13.	13.
14.	14.
15.	15.

Cliché or Proverb

A cliché or proverb is a common saying that conveys a message or idea.
Example: Birds of a feather ________________.

☐ drift apart ☐ flock together

Just from looking at the context clue "birds of a feather," you know that all the birds are similar.

Directions: Read each proverb/cliché. Select the correct answer based on the context clues provided.

1. Make it plain and _____________.

   ☐ confusing ☐ simple

2. You never know until you __________. If you don't try, you can only speculate on what might have happened.

   ☐ don't try ☐ try

3. Absence makes the heart grow ______________.

   ☐ crazy ☐ fonder

4. Sneaky as a _________.

   ☐ potato pie ☐ snake

5. A man is known by the ____________ he keeps. Surround yourself with people you admire and respect.

   ☐ enemies ☐ company

6. An apple a day keeps ______________.

   ☐ you at the doctor ☐ the doctor away

7. Beggars ________ be choosers.

   ☐ can ☐ can't

8. Blood is thicker than ____________.

   ☐ ketchup ☐ water

9. Curiosity __________ the cat.

   ☐ rebirthed ☐ killed

10. Do unto others as you ___________them to do unto you.

    ☐ want ☐ wouldn't want

Directions: Read each proverb/cliché. From reading the context clues in the sentence, select the correct answer.

1. Crime _____ pay. Any gains are short-term and the consequences, if caught, are life shattering.
☐ does ☐ does not

2. Trust me, I am not the best role model. Do as I say and ________ as I do.
☐ exactly ☐ not

3. _____________ is the best teacher because you can learn what or what not to do.
☐ Lack of experience ☐ Experience

4. A fool and his money are ____________________. Save and invest wisely.
☐ never parted ☐ soon parted

5. ____________ speak louder than words. It is often easier to say than to do.
☐ No action ☐ Actions

6. Do you really want to know? I am honest, so ask me questions and I'll tell _________ lies.
☐ no ☐ all

7. _______________ correctly makes perfect.
☐ Guessing ☐ Practicing

8. A man is ________ by his friends. If your friends constantly lie, cheat, and steal, I will assume that you'll do the same.
☐ not known ☐ known

9. This math problem is all wrong. You need to start from___________.
☐ scratch ☐ the end

10. Appearances _____ deceiving. Looks can be deceiving, so take your time in getting to know someone.
☐ can be ☐ are never

Homonyms and Context Clues

Homonyms are words that are pronounced the same yet spelled differently. The words have different meanings. **Example:** which and witch

Directions: Read each sentence below and select the correct answer.

1. She took her time to __________ the letter. She wanted to choose the ________words.

   right write wright rite

2. His only ___________in the play was to _________down the hill.

   rear roll roam role

3. Regardless of how bad the __________ gets, I must decide __________ to go to the party.

   whether than then weather

4. You must use the ________ to row the boat, __________ we will remain in one spot.

   ore or oar would

5. The _________came into our room and __________the bed.

   bear made bare maid

6. The ___________was ___________because of their fighting.

   medal band banned metal

7. The __________went by so fast that she felt as if she were in a __________.

   heel daze heal days

8. For her ___________to _____________, she needed to keep her foot elevated.

   coarse heal course heel

9. He made some biscuits with the ___________. Then, he went outside to pick a ____________to put into the vase.

   fined flower find flour

10. She began to write all her numbers, including number __________, on the board. After seeing her, I wanted to write, __________.

    too slay to two

11. The ___________in her forehead bulged out very far. She was very __________ and angered quickly when others got attention for their appearance.

    vane vain stair vein

12. On ___________, Sue went to the ice cream store to buy a __________.

stationary   Sunday   sundae   stationery

13. You need to go ahead and _________the presents. Then, turn off that _______ music!

wave   waive   wrap   rap

14. The __________ from the chimney turned his _________black.

sum   suit   some   soot

15. She ___________her book while ironing her ___________dress for school.

rein   red   rain   read

16. Since I couldn't ride on my ___________ bike, I went to get some ___________ to write a letter.

seize   stationery   sees   stationary

17. Although he will ____________ you to your face, remember that he ______________ on small weaknesses.

prays   prints   praise   preys

18. Despite her dog's comforting _______________touching her leg, she was so nervous that she had to _______________before speaking.

patience   pause   paws   patients

19. She knew that some of her obligations and chores were _______________, but the doctor told her that she needed to take it easy and not _______________ it.

mustered   overdue   mustard   overdo

Homonyms

Directions: Select the correct definition.

1. wait
☐ serve ☐ remain in readiness

2. raze
☐ to lift up ☐ to tear down completely

3. seize
☐ to take ☐ to look

4. principle
☐ head of a school ☐ a rule or standard

5. peek
☐ secret look ☐ top

6. incite
☐ to provoke ☐ within one's view

7. too
☐ toward ☐ also

8. tolled
☐ spoke ☐ rang

9. assent
☐ to agree ☐ go up mountain

10. coarse
☐ path ☐ rough

11. tail
☐ extension from an animal's behind ☐ story

12. week
☐ not strong ☐ seven days

13. scent
☐ send away ☐ smell

14. steel
☐ to take away ☐ piece of metal

Homographs

Homographs are words that are spelled the same but have different meanings.

Example: The baby burped a lot because she had a lot of gas.

We need to stop and put some gas in the car.

Other Examples:

1. stick

   Put the stick down.

   He decided to stick with her, despite her troubles.

2. grade

   The teacher had to grade the papers.

   She is in the first grade.

3. park

   We went to the park to play.

   You need to park the car.

4. check

   We wrote a check to cover the charges.

   We need to check on Lily. She is not feeling well.

5. stone

   She had a stone look on her face.

   The stone in her ring was beautiful.

6. club

   They went to the club to dance.

   She hit the man in the head with a club.

7. hammer

   We brought a hammer to build the cabinet.

   We have to hammer it down tight.

8. voice

   Why can't I voice my opinion?

   She had a beautiful singing voice.

9. wave

   The ocean wave was so high, it scared her.

   She raised her hand to wave bye to her friend.

10. notice
   She received notice that she had to move immediately.
   Did you notice that she was not smiling?

11. fit
   I feel fit enough to run ten miles.
   I can still fit into my size 10 dresses.

12. watch
   What time do you have on your watch?
   What do you want to watch on television?

13. bowl
   Do you like to bowl for fun?
   Mix all the ingredients in the bowl.

14. tap
   Her favorite form of dance is tap.
   I prefer water out of the tap to bottled water.

15. glasses
   He took the clean glasses from the dishwasher.
   She took her glasses off to rub her eye.

16. bow
   We walked to the bow of the ship.
   She put a yellow bow in her hair.

17. train
   Instead of driving, I will take the train to work.
   You need to train your dog to obey you.

18. strike
   They went on strike for better wages.
   She didn't mean to strike the child.

19. bark
   The squirrel ran up the bark of the tree.
   I heard the dog bark late last night.

20. punch
   May I have some punch with my cake?
   She took a punch at him because she was so angry.

Compound Words

A compound word is made when two words are joined to form a new word.
Example: Look at the words below. Which word is a compound word? Why?

☐ tiredness ☐ amazement ☐ myself ☐ faithful

* The answer is the word <u>myself</u>. <u>Myself</u> is a compound word because the words <u>my</u> and <u>self</u> are two separate words. When they are combined, they make one new word.

Directions: Look at the words below. Put an X in the box by the compound word.

1. ☐ began ☐ turnaround ☐ hopeful ☐ relations
2. ☐ already ☐ battlefield ☐ regain ☐ untapped
3. ☐ began ☐ reborn ☐ amusement ☐ paperclip
4. ☐ crackdown ☐ scanner ☐ blindly ☐ gopher
5. ☐ intercom ☐ passerby ☐ liability ☐ present
6. ☐ engineering ☐ cupful ☐ piggyback ☐ weekly
7. ☐ masterpiece ☐ supportive ☐ imagery ☐ hurriedly
8. ☐ pioneer ☐ remain ☐ pileup ☐ diverse
9. ☐ commitment ☐ layover ☐ founder ☐ retired
10. ☐ downsize ☐ owner ☐ relative ☐ believer
11. ☐ university ☐ organization ☐ twofold ☐ blindly
12. ☐ mastermind ☐ coincidence ☐ quickly ☐ progress
13. ☐ introduce ☐ stapler ☐ farfetched ☐ computerized
14. ☐ corkscrew ☐ amusement ☐ semester ☐ resemblance
15. ☐ buoy ☐ homestretch ☐ realness ☐ evolution
16. ☐ foreign ☐ disloyal ☐ drawbridge ☐ cynic

17. ☐ calculation ☐ falter ☐ expression ☐ aftermath

18. ☐ eyesore ☐ trivial ☐ renounce ☐ havoc

19. ☐ disheveled ☐ avid ☐ coastline ☐ atmosphere

20. ☐ alien ☐ dingy ☐ confide ☐ skateboard

21. ☐ worthwhile ☐ considerate ☐ strategy ☐ random

22. ☐ somber ☐ guideline ☐ fossil ☐ dissect

23. ☐ exercise ☐ tornado ☐ waterproof ☐ arrangement

24. ☐ language ☐ logical ☐ narrative ☐ shortchange

25. ☐ comprehensive ☐ proofread ☐ objective ☐ howling

26. ☐ mountainside ☐ tomorrow ☐ structure ☐ statements

27. ☐ quietly ☐ request ☐ trustworthy ☐ variety

28. ☐ yardstick ☐ advanced ☐ discussions ☐ details

29. ☐ economy ☐ popularity ☐ modify ☐ footprint

30. ☐ tallest ☐ weeklong ☐ expand ☐ shutter

31. ☐ reverses ☐ swallowing ☐ hotheaded ☐ mixture

32. ☐ preacher ☐ birdbrain ☐ detective ☐ mechanics

33. ☐ eyeballs ☐ collective ☐ equipment ☐ champion

34. ☐ handling ☐ eliminate ☐ heavyweight ☐ striving

35. ☐ ripens ☐ menace ☐ details ☐ quicksand

Compound Words

Directions: Use words from the word bank to form compound words.

still	web	work	outs
storm	skate	less	box
brush	stood	stock	fly
lid	trodden	shelf	thinker
ship	struck	ache	fallen

1. under________________

2. awe________________

3. hope________________

4. down________________

5. laughing________________

6. head________________

7. book________________

8. butter________________

9. free________________

10. paint________________

11. mail________________

12. crest________________

13. cheap________________

14. try________________

15. stand________________

16. home________________

17. eye________________

18. cob________________

19. citizen________________

20. brain________________

Matching Definitions

Directions: Match the words in the word box to its definition. The first one is done for you.

fate	unison	suffice	attain
abreast	oblivious	chirpy	hostile
whim	novice	strewed	frequent

agonized	scarce	undaunted
extracurricular	rational	accentuated

1. full of defiance - hostile

2. destiny -

3. speak in lively way -

4. emphasized -

5. in concord; harmony -

6. sufficient or adequate -

7. side by side -

8. outside of the regular curriculum -

9. to achieve -

10. not faltering or hesitating -

11. forgetful, unmindful, or unaware -

12. struggled; anguished -

13.something that happens often -

14. new or inexperienced -

15. reasonable thought -

16. scattered -

17. insufficient amount -

18. idle or passing notion –

Connotations

The denotation of a word provides a specific meaning. Basically, it is the dictionary definition of a word. The connotation of a word refers to the associations that are connected to that word. Connotations can be positive, as well as negative.

Review the examples in the box below.

Positive Denotations with Negative Connotations

1. confident- arrogant	6. empty – abandoned
2. relaxed - lazy	7. proper - prissy
3. slim - bony	8. ordinary - homely
4. yelled - shrieked	9. persuade - brainwash
5. laugh - cackle	10. unaware - ignorant

As stated above, connotations can be positive. Contrast the connotations below. Even though neither connotation is negative, there is still a difference in how each term is perceived.

1. pretty – eye catching	6. skinny - slender
2. shiny - lustrous	7. stink - aroma
3. woman - lady	8. tiny - petite
4. laugh - giggle	9. interested - fascinated
5. raw - natural	10. different - distinct

Connotations

Directions: Look at the words in each set below. Underline the word in each set with the most positive connotation.

Examples: <u>detective</u>, eavesdropper, spy, wiretapper

Detective would be underlined because it is the most positive.

1. lounge, lazy, goof off, bum
2. colorful, loud, bright, blinding
3. inarticulate, dumb, idiotic, stupid
4. raging, furious, angry, irate
5. agreeable, push-over, sap, doormat
6. child-like, immature, infantile, youthful
7. wail, cry, howl, squall
8. gossip, babble, talk, blab
9. crazy, unique, eccentric, unusual
10. guest, intruder, interloper, visitor
11. content, smug, egomaniac, self-centered
12. tread, squash, tramp, overwhelm
13. peculiar, eccentric, unique, quirky
14. evaporated, parched, dehydrated, shriveled
15. argue, debate, fuss, confront
16. ask, pry, delve, interrogate
17. welt, inflammation, swelling, blister
18. smart, egghead, nerd, geek
19. stimulate, instigate, wheedle, provoke
20. stubborn, defiant, resolute, hard-headed

Connotations

Directions: Each of the following sentences includes a pair of words with similar dictionary definitions, but different connotations. Put an X in the box with the correct connotation.

1. She was so _____________around his dog that he put the dog outside.
☐ prudish ☐ squeamish

2. The girl tried to ___________ out the sour candy.
☐ spit ☐ eject

3. Mary Ann was so ___________________ that she sat in the back of the class so that she wouldn't have to talk to anyone.
☐ bashful ☐ reserved

4. The dog ________________ in pain when he got his shots.
☐ yelped ☐ barked

5. She was so _______________ that she tripped over the stool.
☐ gawky ☐ clumsy

6. The _______________ of the accident demolished both cars.
☐ shock ☐ impact

7. You could see through the glass, for the house was __________________.
☐ unsullied ☐ immaculate

8. We had a diverse group of people at Billy's ___________________________.
☐ party ☐ high tea

9. The teen was so out of control that some people viewed him as being ______________.
☐ negligent ☐ delinquent

10. The employees decided to ________________ due to low wages.
☐ blockade ☐ picket

11. Ever since the book fell on his head, he has suffered memory ______________.
☐ reversions ☐ lapses

12. She was so ______________ that she thought that she was better than everyone else.
☐ conceited ☐ boastful

13. Even though the knife ________________ his lung, he survived.
☐ sliced ☐ punctured

14. The house was ________________ by the floodwaters.
☐ destroyed ☐ devoured

15. In the spring, our flowers started _______________.
☐ vegetating ☐ budding

16. Ignoring my sign, the man _________________ onto my property.
☐ invaded ☐ trespassed

17. Even though he had a job, he was called a _____________ since he hid from all work.
☐ wanderer ☐ loafer

18. He looked so ____________ that it seemed as if a slight wind could topple him.
☐ inferior ☐ puny

19. The _____________ from the bank caused considerable stress.
☐ defrauding ☐ theft

20. To _____________ him, she sent her son to his room.
☐ sentence ☐ punish

21. He looked very __________________ at his retirement ceremony.
☐ stiffed-necked ☐ dignified

Connotations

Directions: Read each sentence. Make a new sentence by changing the underlined connotation to a new word. Select a new word from the box below. The first one is done for you.

immature	reckless	despicable
argues	egotistical	truant
hostile	unforgiving	uncertainty
deception	unfit	penalized
impact	pressured	disorderly

1. She talks constantly.

She argues constantly.

2. Her plans were unclear to me.

Her plans were ____________________ to me.

3. You could see the look of despair in his eyes.

You could see the look of ____________________ in his eyes.

4. The man's actions were so lame that I felt sick.

The man's actions were so ____________________ that I felt sick.

5. The plans were doomed from the start because the conditions were unfavorable.

The plans were doomed from the start because the conditions were ________________.

6. She directed everyone to sit down and listen.

She ____________________ everyone to sit down and listen.

7. Her lies were cruel as well as vindictive.

Her lies were cruel as well as ____________________.

8. She was always absent from school.

She was always ____________________ from school.

9. His trick did not work, for she immediately knew that he was lying.

His ____________________did not work, for she immediately knew that he was lying.

10. Linda was so unpredictable that she was fired the second day.

Linda was so ____________________ that she was fired the second day.

11. The bump made him hit his head on the pavement.

The ____________________ made him hit his head on the pavement.

12. He was punished by being made to sit in time-out.

He was ____________________ by being made to sit in time-out.

13. She was so self - seeking that it was irritating to be around her.

She was so ____________________ that it was irritating to be around her.

14. Dehydration made him unable to complete the race.

Dehydration made him ____________________to complete the race.

15. Losing the contest made him feel sad.

Losing the contest made him feel ____________________.

Connotations

Directions: Circle the word with the most negative connotation.

1 dreamy preoccupied absent-minded

2. scent rancid smell

3. vintage antique outdated

4. bother torment tease

5. preoccupied inattentive delirious

6. youthful childish lively

7. self-confident assured vain

8. persuade argue convince

9. accidental forgetful negligent

10. gossip chat converse

Directions: Circle the word with the most positive connotation.

11. sneered smiled smirked

12. shy timid meek

13. economical cheap cut-rate

14. smug superior assured

15. stubborn determined headstrong

16. eager impatient anxious

17. squabble quarrel discussion

18. prying inquisitive nosey

19. bold cocky brash

20. interrogated questioned challenged

Connotations

Directions: Match the words in the word box to its match. The first one is done for you.

stagger	reprimand	whack	destitute
gossip	ill-mannered	useless	
homebody	unsympathetic	wrath	
scorn	unfeeling	shriek	
blemish	obsess	thrifty	

1. yell - shriek

2. hit -

3. underprivileged -

4. fury -

5. haunt -

6. frugal -

7. futile -

8. chastise -

9. misbehaved –

10. rumor -

11. numb -

12. weave -

13. mock -

14. recluse -

15. ruthless -

16. stain -

Directions: Underline the two words or phrases in each group that are opposite in meaning to the underlined vocabulary word.

1. reality realism falsity realness fiction

2. crucial important immaterial relevant irrelevant

3. succumb yield perish survive make it

4. capable unable resourceful susceptible able

5. undaunted shaken cowardly determined unshaken

6. resounding ringing quiet weakening reverberating

7. sophisticated naïve cultivated gullible educated

8. fashionable stylish frumpy faddish dowdy

9. expert proficient unskilled adept unprofessional

10. concluded ended unfinished terminated began

11. resplendent ugly glorious colorless splendid

12. oblivious unmindful mindful observant unaware

13. affirm contradict confirm negate support

14. enhanced decreased reduced increased intensified

15. defiant compliant resistant easygoing insubordinate

16. deteriorated recuperate crumble worsen recovered

17. hostile amicable unthreatening bitter belligerent

18. challenging easy difficult thought-provoking boring

19. glowing dull bright luminous unenthusiastic

20. wisdom wise sensible folly foolishness

21. lush little plush abundant scarce

Vocabulary

Directions: Choose the correct word from the word box to complete each of the following sentences. Some of the words will not be used.

intensity	survival	intricacy	crucial	distinguished
pressured	comprehend	fate	desperately	impact
disillusioned	goal	whim	succumb	far-fetched
compelled	endeavors	obstacles	potential	awestruck
agonized	pact	reflection	abreast	reality

1. She _____________________ wanted to win the prize.

2. It was _____________________ that he took his medication.

3. She felt _____________________to speak out against what she believed was wrong.

4. He didn't want to _____________________ to fatigue, so he took a small break.

5. Since he took a gamble on a _____________________, he lost everything.

6. They made a _____________________that they would be friends forever.

7. She felt _____________________over losing the contest.

8. The _____________________of the harsh words caused her to fall into a depression.

9. The _____________________ of the flames caused the firefighters to move back.

10. He has the _____________________to achieve all his dreams.

11. He knew that his only chance of _____________________ was to grab the rope.

12. Even though she was capable of making good grades, she felt _____________________ to act like she wasn't smart.

13. The boy was _____________________ at how pretty she was.

14. The lie was so _____________________that no one believed him.

15. She could not _____________________ the magnitude of the problem.

16. Her _____________________ in the mirror made her smile.

17. Her _____________________was to win the contest.

18. She did not want to believe the _____________________of the situation.

19. The _____________________ were so great that she felt like giving up.

20. The _____________________of the puzzle caused her to give up.

21. She refused to accept her _____________________ because she wanted to win.

22. She _____________________ over her decision so much that she became tired.

Vocabulary

Directions: Choose the correct word from the list below to complete each of the following sentences. Some of the words will not be used.

coincidence	extracurricular	disbelieving	exhaustion
practically	numerous	extraordinary	gratitude
resounding	undaunted	smug	intimidate
criteria	unfamiliar	fashionable	disclose
expert	growth	credible	

1. Since she was an ____________________in the subject matter, they hired her.

2. There were ______________________ mistakes in her homework.

3. She had a ____________________ look on her face because she was sure that she had won.

4. It was no ____________________ that he was seated at the same table as his secret admirer.

5. He looked very ____________________in his new suit.

6. Because of her ____________________, she fainted after the race.

7. He was ____________________by the jeers of the crowd.

8. Her test results were ____________________ compared to other students.

9. The ____________________noise caused her ears to ache.

10. He felt ____________________ toward the judges for choosing him.

11. The ____________________ for winning were not clear.

12. He tried to ____________________ her by blocking her path.

13. Her ____________________ activities caused her to fall behind in her grades.

14. Her ____________________spurt caused her to grow two inches in three months.

15. She had ____________________won the contest but lost in the last few seconds.

Vocabulary

Directions: Choose the correct word from the list below to complete each of the following sentences. Some of the words will not be used.

oblivious	burdensome	overwhelming	emphasis	exterior	sarcastically
visualize	anticipation	tense	glisten	admiration	attain
disguise	encounter	vaguely	compensated	sketch	
perturbed	comparison	concluded	gleam	reassured	

1. She didn't know all the problems that she would ________________________.

2. More ________________________ was placed on talent than beauty.

3. She ________________________ that the main cause of the problem was Eric.

4. The dew on the grass made it ________________________.

5. She was ________________________ at his disruptive behavior.

6. The arguments caused everyone to become ________________________.

7. He ____________________remarked that she wouldn't have won if he hadn't tripped.

8. To become a winner, you must first ________________________ yourself as one.

9. His ________________________of the gang leader caused him to make wrong choices.

10. Even though the interior of the house looked good, the _________________was worn.

11. Her problems were so ________________________ that she cried a lot.

12. She ________________________ him that everything would be fine.

13. Because of his ________________________, no one recognized him.

14. She was ________________________ to the dangers that she faced.

15. In ________________________ of the money she was to receive, she went shopping.

16. In ________________________ to the other job, this job pays more.

17. She was determined to ________________________ her goals.

18. The incident happened so long ago that she _______________ remembered the details.

Vocabulary

Directions: Choose the correct word from the list below to complete each of the following sentences. Some of the words will not be used.

proceeded	bleak	affirming	etched	cease
odds	hindrance	clarify	insistence	drastic
duped	mingle	status	complacent	swarmed
discipline	primarily	popularity	achievers	challenge
prospects	possibilities	suffice	adjustment	unison

1. The cheerleaders cheered in __________________________.

2. She did not understand the directions, so she asked him to _________________________.

3. Exercising was a big ____________________________for her since she hated doing it.

4. She didn't want to _____________________________because she was shy.

5. The bees ______________________________around the flowers.

6. They slowly ____________________________to the finish line.

7. She had a big ________________________________ to make in her new job.

8. A lot of people were __________________________by the con man.

9. It takes a lot of ___________________________ to exercise consistently.

10. The ___________________________were against them from the very beginning.

11. They were all ___________________________, for they made the honor roll.

12. Due to the ________________________________ of his mom, Ben hired a tutor.

13. He won ________________________________through cheating.

14. Winning the game looked _______________because they were behind by twenty points.

15. Since she had high test scores, the _________________of going to college looked good.

16. The storm didn't ____________________________until five hours later.

17. Her friends were a ______________________________to her.

18. Because she had lost many pounds, her weight loss was too _______________________.

19. His __________________________________ as class president was unchallenged.

20. Juan's ____________________ caused him to believe that he was better than his friends.

21. There are many _____________________________________in your career choice.

22. Due to her _____________________________ statements, Betty felt that she could achieve her dreams.

Vocabulary

Directions: Choose the correct word from the list below to complete each of the following sentences. Some of the words will not be used.

hostile	accentuated	cushioned	glowing	awaited	perspective
gloat	deteriorated	burden	procession	viewed	strewed
appearance	challenging	despair	vast	encased	vanishing
wisdom	forthcoming	influence	flinch	emerge	lush
tumultuous	swirled	enhanced	possess	defiant	antique

1. The wedding ____________________moved slowly.

2. The leaves ____________________around the yard.

3. Her ____________________on the situation was different from his.

4. He left his clothes ____________________around the room.

5. Her mind ____________so quickly that it was difficult for her to remember things.

6. His friends had such a great __________ on him that he couldn't make decisions on his own.

7. The grass was ____________________ and green.

8. Even though she felt pain, she did not ____________________.

9. The furniture was so old that it was considered ____________________.

10. The light was ____________________ so brightly that it made her eyes hurt.

11. The environment was so ____________________ that they began to feel tense.

12. The dress ____________________ her figure.

13. They ____________________the other team as losers.

14. Algebra was very ____________________ to her.

15. She felt ____________________ because everything was going wrong.

16. The child was very ____________________and determined to do it his way.

17. Her ____________________made her look older than she really was.

18. Even though she was only fifteen, she had the __________ of a much older person.

19. The mountain was ____________________ in comparison to the smaller hills.

20. Her grades ____________________ her chances of getting into a good college.

21. His chances of making the football team were ____________________before him.

22. Working two jobs became a ____________________ because she was always tired.

Commonly Confused Words

Directions: When two words have similar sounds or spellings, it can be confusing! Write the correct word to complete each sentence.

choose chose

1. It was difficult for her to ________________ a gift. Finally, she ________________a gift card.

lose loose

2. He did not mean to ________________ his belt. Now his pants are ________________ without his belt.

and an

3. She wanted cookies ________________ candy. But her mom told her to eat ________________ apple.

wonder wander

4. Even though I was told not to ________________ by my mom, I did so anyway. Now I ________________ how to find her in the crowded store.

emigrated immigrated

5. Upon adulthood, he ________________ from the Middle East to the United States. A few years later, his parents ________________ too.

stationery stationary

6. For exercise, she rides her ________________ bike in her basement. While riding her bike, she noticed that she needed more ________________ paper.

coarse course

7. Sue enrolled in a sewing ________________. In her first class, she learned about ________________ material.

effect   affect

8. The loud music outside Jean's window did ________________her ability to sleep. The next day, Jean's neighbor apologized for any ________________ his loud music had on her.

capital   Capitol

9. Washington D.C. is the ________________of the United States. In D.C., the U.S. Congress meet in the building named the United States __________________.

clothes   cloths

10. You need to iron your ___________________. Afterwards, dust the furniture with the new _____________________.

forth   fourth

11. Can we please move ___________________to get the job done? This is the _____________________time we had a delay.

brought   bought

12. At the store, she _____________________ herself a beautiful pastel dress to wear to the party. The salesperson ____________________it to her in a plastic bag for transport.

compliment   complement

13. The tie ___________________ his suit. At the party, he received lots of _____________________.

precede   proceed

14. Because Dan did not know the right route, Lily told him to ___________________ to the first walkway. To see if he knew the route back, Lily told Dan that he could _______________________ her.

lie lay

15. Please ________________the book down. Afterwards, go and ________________ down and take a nap.

too to

16. Please go ________________ bed. Today has been ________________ hectic and you should be tired.

collaborate corroborate

17. To prove or disapprove the theory, we must ______________________ to meet the deadline. If everything proves to be true, our focus should be to ______________________ the theory with our evidence.

who whom

18. ________________ is going to the park with me? I am going to meet a group of friends ______________________ I have known for many years.

fewer less

19. Because of his strict practice sessions, Reggie found that he was making ____________________ mistakes. However, he learned that some weeks he could do with ________________________ practice.

buy by

20. I had to go to the store to ________________some fruit. I stopped ________________ the bank to withdraw some money.

Context Clues

Context clues are hints used to assist readers in understanding unknown words. Context clues may be in the same sentence as the unknown words or in sentences that come before or after them.
Example: Jewel purposefully spilled her drink on Tanya. To not get in trouble, she pretended it was an accident.

You can conclude the word purposefully means planned because Jewel pretended it was an accident.

Directions: Choose the correct word to complete each of the following sentences. Use context clues to find the meaning of the underlined words.

1. Since all the evidence was inconclusive, the charges were dropped due to insufficient evidence.
☐ provable ☐ circumstantial ☐ verifiable

2. The smell penetrated the whole house. We had to open all the windows.
☐ entered ☐ exited ☐ halfway through

3. She was renowned in her community for being an excellent and popular singer.
☐ unfamiliar ☐ celebrated ☐ criticized

4. Even though we tried to shield her from his lies, she was soon exposed to them.
☐ expose ☐ safeguard ☐ uncover

5. His plans were so obscure that she urged him to make them more defined.
☐ clear ☐ plain ☐ vague

6. He was known as a liar, so she was reluctant to trust him.
☐ eager ☐ unwilling ☐ ready

7. Even though she didn't realize it, her life was in jeopardy because of the risk of falling rocks.
☐ danger ☐ valid ☐ side

8. Using her charm, she beguiled him into believing all her lies.
☐ expose ☐ misled ☐ revealed

9. Instead of rushing to decide, she took her time to ponder the situation.
☐ consider ☐ ignore ☐ disregard

10. He made such a rash decision that he felt foolish afterwards.
☐ cautionary ☐ hurried ☐ careful

11. It was such a wintry day that we stayed in to drink hot chocolate and snuggle by the fire.
☐ windy ☐ warm ☐ chilly

12. The animals ravaged the garden leaving only weeds.
☐ ruined ☐ saved ☐ protected

13. Her outfit was so striking that she received many compliments.
☐ ordinary ☐ remarkable ☐ unattractive

14. Because of his bad reputation and being known as an outcast, no one talked to him.
☐ outsider ☐ insider ☐ employee

15. She was prudent with her money because she was saving to buy a car.
☐ hasty ☐ careless ☐ careful

16. She kept knocking my books down to provoke me.
☐ aggravate ☐ avoid ☐ pacify

17. The teacher had to reprimand her for being continually late to class.
☐ compliment ☐ punish ☐ praise

18. The pain began to lessen as the medication took effect.
☐ diminish ☐ intensify ☐ magnify

Context Clues

Directions: Choose the one word or phrase that best keeps the meaning of the underlined word.

> Sarah did not want to get into an altercation with Mary. Whenever she saw Mary, she went out of her way to avoid her.

1. Select the meaning of the word altercation.
☐ reconcile ☐ heated argument ☐ friendly debate

> The colicky baby cried and cried. The father tried his best to pacify the baby by whatever means necessary.

2. Select the meaning of the word pacify.
☐ soothe ☐ enrage ☐ provoke

> Lila knew something was wrong with Devin's insistence that they should be friends. She was finally able to discern that he was only after her money.

3. Select the meaning of the word discern.
☐ ignore ☐ overlook ☐ recognize

> The lawyer knew the witness was not telling the truth. He was finally able to invalidate his claims through the testimony of one eyewitness.

4. Select the meaning of the word invalidate.
☐ support ☐ prove false ☐ prove true

> Because she had an amiable personality, it was easy for her to make friends. No matter where she went, people were drawn to her.

5. Select the meaning of the word amiable.
☐ disagreeable ☐ friendly ☐ aloof

Laughing, Billy stepped on the girl's toe as he ran past her. The girl was astonished by his level of disrespect.

6. Select the meaning of the word astonished.
☐ unruffled ☐ shocked ☐ indifferent

Patricia couldn't understand why Dave was still angry. She felt that their argument was just a petty misunderstanding.

7. Select the meaning of the word petty.
☐ mammoth ☐ small ☐ enormous

Even though she was a natural athlete, her zeal to win caused her to cheat. Due to this, she was disqualified from the last race.

8. Select the meaning of the word zeal.
☐ disinterest ☐ indifference ☐ determination

Beatrice had excellent study habits. She was staunch in her beliefs that good study habits would help her earn good grades.

9. Select the meaning of the word staunch.
☐ steadfast ☐ wavering ☐ fluctuating

He hated his job. The work was too tedious. He was tired of doing the same thing over and over, day in and day out.

10. Select the meaning of the word tedious.
☐ boring ☐ exciting ☐ interesting

They denounced him because of his evil ways.

11. Select the meaning of the word denounced.
☐ applauded ☐ condemned ☐ flattered

Spelling Rules

To become a better speller, there are certain rules that you should remember. Vowels are A, E, I, O, U, and sometimes Y.

Consonants are all letters of the alphabet that are not vowels. Consonants are B, C, D, F, G, H, J, K, L, M, N, P, Q, R, S, T, V, W, X, Z, and sometimes Y .

Y may be a consonant or a vowel.

Rule #1: I before e, except after c, or when pronounced ay as in freight.

Examples of I before e: believe, achieve
Examples of words sounded as ay: weight, freight
Exceptions to this rule: receive, receipt

The Plural of Nouns

Rule #2: When a noun is singular, add s to the ending to make plural.

Examples: computer = computers
guitar = guitars
nickel = nickels
computer = computers

Rule #3: When a singular noun ends in s, sh, ch, or x, add es to the ending to make plural.

Examples: glass + es = glasses
dish + es = dishes
match + es = matches
box + es = boxes

Rule 4: When a singular noun has a consonant before the final y, delete the y and replace it with ies at the ending to make plural.

Examples: cherry = cherries
city = cities
hobby = hobbies
penny = pennies

Rule #5: When a singular noun has a vowel before the final y, add s to the ending to make plural.

Examples: monkey = monkeys
key = keys
day = days
essay = essays

Rule #6: In some cases, when a singular noun ends in f or fe, add a s to the ending to make plural.

Examples: tradeoff + s = tradeoffs
giraffe+ s = giraffes
mischief + s = mischiefs
café + s = cafes

Rule #7: In some cases, when a singular noun ends in f, or fe, delete the f or fe and add ves to the ending to make plural.

Examples: thief + ves = thieves
wolf + ves = wolves
knife + ves = knives
wife + ves = wives

Rule #8: When a singular noun is compound (more than one word), add a s to the ending of the principal word to make plural.

Examples: passer + by = passers-by
sister + in + law = sisters-in-law
runner + up = runners-up

Rule #9: When a singular noun is compound (more than one word), and ends in ful, add a s to the ending to make plural.

Examples: basket + ful = basketfuls
mouth + ful = mouthfuls
hand + ful = handfuls

Rule #10: Some nouns are the same in the singular and plural form.

Examples: She packed one piece of luggage for the trip.
They packed 7 pieces of luggage for the trip.

Could you please move this piece of furniture to the basement?
Could you please move all the furniture to both rooms?

One sheep wandered away from the barn.
Many sheep wandered away from the barn.

Jill caught one fish.
Jill caught many fish.

Spelling Rules (Consonants and Vowels)

Rule #11: In some cases, keep the final e if the suffix begins with a consonant.

Examples: peace + ful = peaceful
state + hood = statehood
forgive + ness = forgiveness

** There are exceptions to Rule #11.

Examples: true + ly = truly
argue + ment = argument
acknowledge + ment = acknowledgment

Rule #12: In some cases, delete the final e if the suffix begins with a vowel.

Examples: admire +ation = admiration
hope + ing = hoping
imagine + ary = imaginary

** There are exceptions to Rule #12.

Examples: like + able = likeable
canoe + ing = canoeing
outrage + ous = outrageous

Spelling

Directions: Read each sentence. Write the correct spelling of the frequently misspelled underlined word. If the underlined word is spelled correctly, write "correct." The first one is done for you.

1. My dad asked me to vacum the carpet. vacuum
2. We had to manever past the cars.
3. I returned the merchandice to the store.
4. We ate at my favorite restarant.
5. They were so exhausted that they flopped on the ground.
6. My competiter was sure that she would win.
7. This was a special occassion.
8. She wrote a weekly column for a newspaper.
9. His tardiness has occured more than once.
10. There's no guaratee that you will win.
11. They were usualy late.
12. You had to get a mininum score of 70% to pass.
13. Everyone could see that the child recklessly running around the store lacked disciapline.
14. Your going to get in trouble if you don't stop.
15. Wanting to tell a more exciting story, she decided to exagerate the situation.
16. Due to his lack of attention, he acidentaly stumbled and fell.
17. It was so cold that all the games were cancelled.
18. Do you realy want to go to the park?
19. All the comitee members voted against the proposal.
20. The do on the grass made it very wet.

Spelling

Directions: Put an X in the box with the correct answer. You may use the dictionary.

1. Whether you ______________ my decision or not, you must abide by it.
☐ except ☐ accept

2. Everyone is going ______________ Dana.
☐ accept ☐ except

3. Before you ______________ any further, you need to talk to Ann.
☐ proceed ☐ precede

4. Since she was the shortest, she ______________ him in line.
☐ proceeded ☐ preceded

5. The dog wagged ______ tail in anticipation.
☐ it's ☐ its

6. _______ so cold outside that she is trembling.
☐ It's ☐ Its

7. They _____________ to the country in which they were born.
☐ emigrated ☐ immigrated

8. They __________________ to a country they had never been.
☐ emigrated ☐ immigrated

9. I need to ___________ down and get some rest.
☐ lie ☐ lay

10. Just ______ the book on the sofa.
☐ lie ☐ lay

11. Make sure you wear gloves because the _______________ may burn your skin.
☐ lie ☐ lye

12. _______ knocking at the door?
☐ Whose ☐ Who's

13. ___________ toy is on the floor?
☐ Whose ☐ Who's

14. We went to the _______where the play was to be held.
☐ cite ☐ site

15. In research papers, you must always ________ where you got your information from.
☐ cite ☐ site

16. _______ the dish down now before you drop it!
☐ Sit ☐ Set

17. You need to _______ down so that other people can see.
☐ sit ☐ set

18. The ____________ to the story is to always be prepared.
☐ morale ☐ moral

19. Her ________ was so low that she didn't try to win.
☐ morale ☐ moral

20. ________ so conniving that it is absolutely sickening.
☐ Your ☐ You're

21. You need to stop _________ yelling.
☐ your ☐ you're

22. Are you going to take my ___________?
☐ advise ☐ advice

23. I would ____________ you to think before you act.
☐ advise ☐ advice

24. He is so _________ at karate that he easily earned his black belt.
☐ good ☐ well

25. Even though he had been in the hospital for a week, he looked __________.
☐ good ☐ well

26. I am so tired that I can't run any ______________.
☐ farther ☐ further

27. Since I don't understand, I will need __________ instructions.
☐ farther ☐ further

28. Her cry ____________ people coming to her aid.
☐ illicited ☐ elicited

29. He was constantly in and out of jail for doing __________ things.
☐ illicit ☐ elicit

30. You have ______________ many clothes in your closet.
☐ too ☐ to

31. You have _____ stop with the negativity.
☐ to ☐ too

Spelling Errors

Directions: Identify the spelling error in each sentence. Underline the error and write the correct spelling of the word. The first one is done for you.

1. She befriended the girls because she really wanted to be populor. popular

2. I want some pie, to.

3. Even though I asked him not to, he decided to move fourth with the project.

4. Sue sold many items at the annaul_bazaar.

5. Brue had all ready gone by the time we made it there.

6. Climbing the ladder to paint the sealing, he saw the windows also needed cleaning.

7. When I moved to a new school, the first person I met was the principle.

8. The pudding is in the dairy isle.

9. Although she wanted to inspire change, she did not want to insight violence.

10. The flower was reel, not artificial.

11. Putting fertilizer on the grass had a positive affect.

13. The artist painted a beautiful seen of the beach.

15. The material was so course that it hurt my skin.

16. He included a acknowledgement in his speech.

17. Please chose between all the items.

18. Could you please go buy the store before coming home?

19. I was hopeing for a more positive outcome.

20. The knife was accidentaly left on the table.

21. Winning the prize was a great acheivement.

22. We were early so we saw the begining.

23. Are you comeing to the party early?

24. The ship finaly docked.

25. We completed our grammer worksheets.

26. Our journey was finaly coming to an end.

27. The comittee members finally decided.

28. The goverment came to a halt.

29. Could you vacum the floor?

30. Did you schedale your appointment?

Single Consonant

The consonants are B, C, D, F, G, H, J, K, L, M, N, P, Q, R, S, T, V, W, X, Z, and sometimes Y.

Directions: Complete each word below with a single consonant.

1. ___opcorn
2. ___-ray
3. ___iography
4. ___ultiply
5. ___ueen
6. ___atient
7. ___cissors
8. ___eight
9. ___ourage
10. ___itchen
11. ___uiz
12. ___emonstrate
13. ___igzag
14. ___eadache
15. ___arbage
16. ___ommunity
17. ___equirement
18. ___righten
19. ___eople
20. ___ocabulary

Double Consonant

Directions: Each word in the left column is misspelled. All are missing a consonant. Correctly spell each word. The first one is done for you. The first one is done for you.

Incorrectly Spelled Word	Doubled Consonant	Correctly Spelled Word
piza	z	pizza
accomodate		
spagheti		
dismis		
compeled		
glosary		
shutle		
hapy		
mispell		
blizard		
cabage		
adition		
folow		
pupet		
peny		
aggresive		
hury		
plumet		
ballon		
colect		
presure		
mudy		
scisors		
arive		
ofice		

Consonant Digraph

A consonant digraph is a sequence of two or more different letters which represents a single sound.

Directions: Complete each word below with a consonant digraph from the box below.

ch wr sh gh kn wh ph th

1. quen______

2. ______ing

3. gra______

4. ______ange

5.______im

6. ______ought

7. ______aplain

8. ______astly

9. smoo______

10. or______an

11. ______eck

12. rewa______

13. ______ot

14. ______erapist

15. ______otographic

16. ______ase

17. fla______

Consonant Digraph

Directions: Complete each word below with a consonant digraph from the box below.

wh th ph ch wr sh ng gh kn wh ph

1. doi______

2. ______arf

3. spri______

4. squa______

5. ______ing

6. ______ead

7. lo______

8. go______er

9. scrat______

10. ______orus

11. ______eory

12. a______

13. sti______

14. ______otty

15. bou______

16. ______imper

17. ______ony

18. ______rub

Consonant Blends

Consonant blends occur when two consonants run into one another or blend and both letters are heard. (Examples: nt, sp, or br)

Directions: Complete each word below with a consonant blend from the box below.

bl	br	cl	cr	dr	fl	fr	gl	gr	ll	pl	pr	sn	st	sp	sc

1. _______owsy
2. _______umsy
3. hu_______
4. _______eam
5. _______ural
6. _______an
7. _______othes
8. _______ecial
9. gra_______
10. _______antic
11. _______azen
12. ga_______
13. _______ade
14. _______ratch
15. _______aw
16. _______enzy
17. _______anket
18. _______ash
19. _______ort

Consonant Blends

Directions: Write "yes" on the blank line to the word that has a consonant blend and "no" if the word doesn't. Underline the consonant blend.

1. threaten
2. eraser
3. holiday
4. shelf
5. against
6. paper
7. breeze
8. hip
9. imagery
10. scream
11. pigeon
12. against
13. penguin
14. pop
15. creature
16. power
17. scurry
18. green
19. complete
20. lamp

Contractions

A contraction is a single word made up of two combined words. You create a contraction by leaving out one or more letters and using an apostrophe in place of the missing letters.

Example: After school, they will go to the park.
Revised with a contraction: After school, they'll go to the park.

Directions: Use the word bank to find and write the contractions for the below words.

don't	I'd	they'd	weren't	won't	you've	I've	o'clock	he'd	isn't
it's	can't	shouldn't	we'd	they're					

1. they are

2. of the clock

3. you have

4. is not

5. do not

6. they would

7. should not

8. I had

9. cannot

10. we would

11. it is

12. were not

13. he would

14. I have

15. will not

Contractions

Directions: There are two words in each sentence that can be combined to make a contraction. Underline the words and write the new contraction.

Example: Who is responsible for putting the drinks on the table?

1. She felt sick because she had eaten too much food to eat.

2. He was too dizzy to stand and could not attend class.

3. Who will go first?

4. KJ must not be late again for practice.

5. They will first have to apologize before coming inside.

6. Before taking the test, you will need to study.

7. It is so cold outside that they brought the animals inside.

8. He had exhausted all options.

9. Before leaving, they had eaten breakfast.

10. At the very least, you have got to try.

11. Because the flowers wilted, I will need to buy more.

12. They would first have to go to the store.

13. Gina ran very fast, but she could not catch up to Pat.

14. We have ten more days before my birthday party.

15. Even though you want to go first, let us wait.

16. Even though I started early, I would need to stay late.

17. Stop now before you are in trouble.

Common Words

Directions: Four of the five words in each group have something in common. Underline the word in each group that doesn't belong. Use the word bank to write what they have in common on the line.

Example: tropical polar <u>beach</u> temperate dry Examples of <u>climate types</u>

live underground	teeth	inventors	fruits	eyes
natural animal habitats	environmental disasters	space	airplane	flowers
tongue	sun	oceans	fast food	map
musical instruments	book genres	computer components	states	baby animals
climate types	puzzles	nouns	insects	sports

1. fantasy science fiction mystery puppetry biography

   Examples of ______________________

2. spiders butterflies grasshoppers ladybugs moths

   Examples of ______________________

3. Artic Lake Huron Indian Pacific Atlantic

   Names of ______________________

4. Violet Daffodil Elm Lily Iris

   Names of ______________________

5. propellor stern cockpit wings rudder

   Parts of ______________________

6. monitor mouse paper keyboard Internet

   Names of ______________________

7. zoo rainforest forest grasslands mountains

   Examples of ______________________

8. bumpy moist organ smooth skeleton

   Describes a ______________________

9. earthquakes rain dust storms floods tornadoes

   Examples of ______________________

10. pupil taste buds cornea retina lashes

    Parts of ______________________

11. chicken nuggets milkshakes buffet hamburgers curly fries

Examples of ______________________

12. pear apple pomegranate mushroom raspberry

Types of ______________________

13. mole locust beaver chipmunk rat

Names of animals/insects that ______________________

14. planets stars comets ocean galaxy

Describe ______________________

15. word search jigsaw landscape crossword sudoku

Kinds of ______________________

16. aurora star heat plankton solar system

Describes ______________________

17. molars opinions quadrants chew thirty-two

Describes ______________________

18. soccer baseball tennis summarize football

Examples of ______________________

19. latitude/longitude lines legend or key scale watch compass rose

Parts of a ______________________

20. eaglet peachick lamb gosling gorilla

Names of ______________________

21. Wyoming Oregon Richmond Arkansas Vermont

Names of ______________________

22. Guitar Electric Clarinet Saxophone Tambourine

Names of ______________________

23. Charles R. Drew, M.D. Anna Connelly Mickey Mouse Thomas Edison George Washington Carver

Names of ______________________

24. Running Person Thing Place Idea

Examples of ______________________

Answer Key

Pages 9 - 12

Using Roots and Affixes

Directions: Knowing the root or affix of a word can help you narrow down the meaning. After reading the root and its meaning, select the best answer.

1. To fracture a leg is to crack it.

2. A democratic government is one that represents the people.

3. The migration of people caused the town to be nearly empty.

4. He was so dehydrated from the lack of water that he nearly fainted.

5. Even though the model had been updated many times, I still preferred the original prototype.

6. Some people believe there is extraterrestrial life in space.

7. Geography is the study of the earth.

8. A benevolent person is one who gives freely and generously.

9. A person who is maladjusted is one who is poorly adjusted.

10. A hexagon has 6 sides.

11. To contradict someone, you speak against him

12. A dermatologist is a doctor who cares for your skin.

13. A gastric disorder is a disorder in the stomach.

14. To magnify means to make bigger.

15. If you have hypertension, you have high blood pressure. If you have hypotension, you have low blood pressure.

16. He decided to be a spectator that cheered for the team.

17. The ship transported us back to the pier.

18. The audience clapped for several minutes.

19. She predicted that her team would win the game.

Page 15

Prefixes

Directions: Complete each word using a prefix from the word bank.

1. impact
2. insignificant
3. binoculars
4. autobiography
5. nonsense
6. postseason
7. submerge
8. incapable
9. misinterpret
10. disbelieved
11. midnight
12. reply
13. predict
14. ness
15. fore, trans, non

Page 16

Prefixes

Directions: Complete each word using a prefix from the word bank.

1. hydrogen
2. microscope
3. automatic
4. thermometer
5. circumstance
6. beneficial
7. propeller
8. semimonthly
9. anticipate
10. triangle
11. temporary
12. chronological
13. quadrilateral
14. aquatic
15. redirect

Pages 17 - 19

Prefixes

Directions: Identify the meaning of the underlined words by using the provided prefixes and context clues.

1. Amphibians can live on land and water.

2. You receive a paycheck biweekly. How often are you paid? every two weeks

3. A semicircle is what percentage of a circle? 50%

4. Even though a microbe is tiny, it can produce disease.

5. Lee loves astronomy because he believes in extraterrestrials. Lee loves to study space.

6. Trixie loves to ride on her tricycle. It has three wheels.

7. An octopus has eight legs.

8. When a person writes an autobiography, he writes about himself.

9. She arrived at the hospital at 8:00 a.m. for preoperative testing. At 12:00 p.m. she was moved to a postoperative room. The 8:00 a.m. testing was before her surgery. She was moved to the postoperative room after the surgery.

10. Quadruple eight. What number do you get? 32

11. How many years are in a century? 100

12. The kids ran the circumference of the yard. They ran completely around the yard.

13. If a company is doing a macroanalysis on why people prefer certain name brands, it is doing a study hefty in scope.

14. A ship moves on top of the water. A submarine moves under the water.

Page 22

Suffixes

Directions: Make a new word by combining the word and suffix. You may have to add or drop some letters. Look at the example below.

1. dangerous
2. famous
3. fashionable
4. usually
5. mountainous
6. practically
7. piteous
8. accidentally
9. favorable
10. admissible
11. logically
12. marvelous
13. assessment
14. abnormally
15. beautifully
16. allegation
17. disposal
18. creative
19. happily
20. perilous

Pages 23 - 24

Suffixes

Directions: Add the correct suffix to the underlined word in each sentence.

1. She was very careless in doing her work. She was in a hurry to go outside.
2. Whenever he didn't get his way, he would act very childish.
3. Even though everyone else looked glum, Dan was cheerful.
4. I didn't believe her story. She just didn't seem truthful.
5. This is the biggest piece of cake I have ever had.
6. Since she was new, she was not comfortable in the school.
7. The party was really awesome.
8. He was a natural artist.
9. Since she showed great responsibility, Tonya was allowed to stay home by herself.
10. His song about love is considered to be beautiful.
11. I am ten feet from the door. Since my teacher is five feet away, she is closer to the door.
12. It took Liz so long to achieve her dream that even she wondered if it would materialize.
13. Be careful when solving your math problems.
14. I love animals so much that I want to study zoology.
15. If you keep picking at your sore, you will get an infection.
16. Since Jean has asthma, she needs an inhaler to help her breathe.
17. She felt feverish, so she checked her temperature with a thermometer.
18. He wanted to take action, rather than to sit around and wait.

Page 25

Suffixes

Directions: Use a suffix from the word bank below to make a word.

1. meaningless
2. acknowledgement
3. trainer
4. dangerous
5. salty
6. approachable
7. realize
8. vengeful
9. comical
10. autograph
11. decorate
12. allergy
13. sadness
14. dutifully
15. spaceship

Page 26

Suffixes

Directions: Use a suffix from the word bank below to make a word.

1. afterward
2. sluggish
3. poverty
4. antibiotic
5. boredom
6. conspiracy
7. magician
8. consequence
9. adulthood
10. spokeswoman
11. awesome
12. counterclockwise
13. frontier
14. sedentary
15. tourist

Page 27

Prefixes and Suffixes

Directions: Add a prefix and/or suffix to each word from the word bank to make two new words. Note: Some prefixes and suffixes may be used more than once.

swirl	swirled	swirling
popular	unpopular	popularity
assure	reassured	reassuring
fashion	unfashionable	fashionable
cap	incapable	uncapable
recognize	recognition	unrecognizable
relent	unrelenting	relenting
possess	possessed	possessing
flinch	flinched	flinching
imagine	unimaginable	imaginary
music	musical	musician
educate	uneducated	miseducate
usual	unusual	unusually
control	controllably	uncontrolled
invent	invented	invention
visible	invisible	visibly
embellish	embellishment	embellished
thrift	thrifty	thriftiest
enchant	enchantment	enchanting

Page 28
Prefixes and Suffixes

Directions: Underline the prefix and/or suffix in each word.

1. designer
2. misspell
3. humorist
4. import
5. kilogram
6. amusement
7. antifreeze
8. postgraduate
9. microscope
10. reverse
11. capable
12. extractor
13. preamble
14. freedom
15. duckling
16. photograph
17. reheat
18. questionable
19. triangle
20. nonfat
21. intake
22. zoology
23. empower
24. lessee
25. internalize
26. uniform

Pages 29 - 30

Prefixes and Suffixes

Directions: Read each paragraph below. Fill in the blank with the correct word.

1. Billy hit another automobile while driving too fast. Instead of waiting for the ambulance to take him to the hospital, he slowly ambled out of his car. He found out later that if his car would have been a manual transmission instead of an automatic, he probably would have died.

2. After not seeing her all day, Jean was wondering why Sue had been absent from school. Sue did not have many friends because she was very quiet and introverted. Due to her antisocial behavior, no one besides Sue wondered if Jean was unwell.

3. It's no fun being excluded from school functions. I don't know why my friends won't include me. It seems as if they only do things to benefit themselves. Nothing that they ever do is beneficial to me.

4. She lies so much that she is known as an untruthful person. She is simply incredible. She constantly forgets what she tells us. She said that she went to Dan's party, although she initially told us that she was sick the night of the party. She often contradicts herself.

5. We sprayed air freshener to deodorize the room. The smell was so unpleasant that we had to open all the windows. The ventilation of the room gradually lessened the disagreeable odor.

6. Our first group project was rejected because of disorganization. Our teacher attributed it to constant infighting. He said the project was a disjointed mess instead of a unified effort.

7. She misinterpreted the directions I gave her. Even though it was her mistake, somehow, she felt that I had misinformed her. Despite her belief, I refuse to completely reconsider her grade. She can rewrite the paper for extra credit if she wants a better grade.

8. The children sat in a semicircle waiting for the semifinal game to start. The children believed the star player to be an extraordinary athlete. The excitement of waiting for him to come on the field and play was unbearable.

9. The paramedics arrived to help the man stuck in his parachute.
They knew that to be successful in helping the man, they had to proceed with caution.

10. Even though she knew her child was hyperactive and undisciplined; James and Charity were hypersensitive to criticism. They finally accepted that something needed to be done after their family staged an intervention.

11. In retrospect, she wished she had done things differently. She faced a multitude of problems, and they seemed to be multiplying daily. Honestly looking back, she realized that it was entirely her fault.

12. Reggie decided that he would not allow Eric, his boss, to disrespect him anymore. An inconsiderate man, Eric would constantly take advantage of Reggie's meek temperament. Although he claimed to accidentally step on Reggie's toes every day, Reggie believed Eric's actions were intentional.

Pages 32-33

Analogies

Directions: Complete the analogies below.

1. zoologist: animals :: archaeologist : fossils

2. amateur: expert :: supporter : adversary

3. site: sight :: here : hear

4. ewe : lamb :: kitten : cat

5. hexagon : 6 :: square : 4

6. pig : piglet :: cow : calf

7. sophisticated : elegant :: ugly : hideous

8. before : prefix :: ending : suffix

9. books : literature :: percentage : math

10. camels : desert :: foxes : forest

11. carnivores : meat eaters :: herbivores : plant eaters

12. pediatrician : child's health care :: optometrist : eye health

13. treadmill : run :: water : swim

14. horses : herd :: geese : gaggle

15. artist : painting :: poet : poetry

16. wings : airplane :: sentence : paragraph

17. error : mistake :: disheveled : rumpled

Page 34

Analogies

Directions: Choose a vocabulary word from the words below to complete each analogy. All words will not be used.

1. spacious : large :: imitate : <u>mimic</u>

2. nonfiction : fiction :: fact : <u>opinion</u>

3. lawn mower : grass :: scythe : <u>wheat</u>

4. peculiar : odd :: standoffish : <u>snobbish</u>

5. water: fish :: land : <u>mammal</u>

6. movie : actors :: story : <u>characters</u>

7. dinosaur : T-Rex :: dog : <u>beagle</u>

8. verb : action :: interjection : <u>emotion</u>

9. ink : pen :: lead : <u>pencil</u>

10. August : noun :: or : <u>conjunction</u>

11. letter : thank you :: report : <u>book</u>

12. bread : bake :: coffee : <u>brew</u>

13. mouth : tongue :: eyes : <u>pupil</u>

14. lion : den :: chicken :: <u>coop</u>

15. knife : cut :: shears : <u>prune</u>

16. degree : temperature :: ounce : <u>weight</u>

Page 35

Analogies

Directions: Choose a vocabulary word from the word bank below to complete each analogy. All words will not be used.

1. woman : baby girl :: goose : gosling
2. scrap : abolish :: necessary : essential
3. century : 100 years :: decade : 10 years
4. dogs : bark :: birds : chirp
5. library : quiet :: football game : loud
6. germs : disease :: carelessness : accidents
7. tulip : flower :: oak : tree
8. lamp : light :: fan : breeze
9. ruthless : brutal :: deterioration : corrosion
10. Richmond : Virginia :: Sacramento : California
11. primary sources : letters :: secondary sources : textbooks
12. plants : seedling :: tree : twigs
13. patience : impatience :: impartial : biased
14. beans : legumes :: milk : dairy
15. choose : chose :: swim : swam
16. clock : time :: thermometer : temperature
17. sleepy : yawn :: itch : scratch
18. hill : mountain :: creek : river

Page 36

Synonyms

Directions: Synonyms are words that have similar meanings. For example, **fall** and **stumble** have similar meanings. Match each word to its synonym in the word bank.

1. old - antique
2. emphasized- accentuated
3. appear - emerge
4. new - modern
5. insubordinate - defiant
6. pained - agonized
7. disappointed - sad
8. radiate - glow
9. unruly - noncompliant
10. buffered- cushioned
11. upset - perturbed
12. impact - influence
13. overpowering - overwhelming
14. revolve - swirl
15. disappoint - frustrate
16. choice - option
17. explain - clarify
18. enclosed - encased

Page 37

Synonyms

Directions: Synonyms – words that have similar meanings. Match each word to its synonym in the word bank.

1. fake - counterfeit
2. cheap - bargain
3. persecute - oppress
4. renew - regenerate
5. sway - rock
6. steady - firm
7. versatile - flexible
8. amiable - good- humored
9. broad - wide
10. contraband - smuggled
11. haggard - worn
12. perky - cheerful
13. sick - unwell
14. skilled - accomplished
15. unscathed - uninjured
16. kick out - expel
17. surge - outpouring
18. remunerate - compensate
19. perplexed - puzzled
20. massive - gigantic
21. kindle - ignite
22. ingest - consume
23. grandiose - impressive
24. fumble - blunder
25. frothy - bubbling

Page 38

Antonyms

Antonyms are words that have opposite meanings. For example, take the word dirty. The opposite of dirty is clean.

Directions: Find the antonym for each word below by choosing a word from the text box below.

1. knowledge - ignorance
2. destroy - create
3. happy - miserable
4. logical - unreasonable
5. nasty- nice
6. withdraw - deposit
7. ancient - young
8. darkened - illuminated
9. feeble - strong
10. grotesque - beautiful
11. dangerous - safe
12. maternal - fatherly
13. neglect - smother
14. peculiar - familiar
15. practical - unrealistic
16. obese - malnourished
17. abundant - scarce
18. luxury - squalor
19. accidental - intentional
20. extinguish - ignite

Page 39

Antonyms

Directions: Match each word to its antonym in the word bank.

1. graceful - clumsy

2. swift - sluggish

3. polite - boorish

4. lead - follow

5. fail - blunder

6. engage - refrain

7. pristine - weathered

8. healthy - ill

9. catch - fumble

10. edible - poisonous

11.miniature - enormous

12. natural - artificial

13. naughty - angelic

14. moist - dry

15. question - answer

16. flexible - rigid

17. enhance - detract

18. grief - joy

19. preserve - destroy

20. restrained - free

21. giving - miserly

22. peaceful - deafening

23. bore - excited

24. enjoy - despise

25. few - infinite

Pages 41 - 42

Idioms

We use idioms in our everyday speech. An idiom is an expression that has a meaning apart from the meaning of its individual words. An idiom should not be taken literally.

1. Nikko did not allow Mr. Perkin's to throw a wet blanket on how he felt.

☐ to encourage him
☐ to discourage him
☐ to provoke him

2. Tiera was dog tired after working with her mom.

☐ unhappy
☐ excited
☐ exhausted

3. Excited to see her best friend perform on stage, he told her to break a leg.

☐ harm herself
☐ hurt someone else
☐ do well

4. Walter thought Annie was yellow - bellied because she didn't want to fight to be a cheerleader.

☐ a fighter
☐ a coward
☐ an instigator

5. Ms. Jenkins had been discouraged year in and year out by students not keeping their promises.

☐ constantly
☐ very seldom
☐ never

6. Wealthy and popular, Laurie felt that she didn't have to work for what she wanted because she was <u>the cream of the crop</u>.

☐ <u>the best</u>
☐ at the bottom of the pack
☐ occasionally winning

7. Betty was not Jason's <u>cup of tea</u> because of differing personalities.

☐ favorite flavor
☐ <u>preference</u>
☐ personal drinking cup

8. Reggie didn't want to talk and <u>beat around the bush</u>.

☐ pruned
☐ jumped in
☐ <u>delay</u>

9. With a few better options, she <u>bit the bullet</u>.

☐ <u>did it despite hesitation</u>
☐ hesitated
☐ bit the bullet for iron

10. Even though Betty had <u>screwed up</u> academically, she was determined that she would make a change.

☐ done a great job
☐ <u>messed up</u>
☐ tightened her screws

Page 43

Idioms

Directions: Read each idiom below. Choose the best word or phrase from the word box that is most similar in meaning. All words/phrases will not be used.

1. raining cats and dogs - raining hard
2. see eye to eye - agree with
3. stuck up - snobbish
4. green with envy - jealous
5. chip on his shoulder - bad attitude; grudge
6. yes man - person that agrees with everything
7. go like clockwork - runs smoothly
8. cut corners - skip steps
9. stick your neck out - take a risk
10. scaredy cat - fearful person
11. all ears - listen carefully
12. egg on - encourage
13. looking out for number one - only caring about himself/herself
14. sunny disposition - happy
15. standing on pins and needles - anxious
16. blind as a bat - unable to see well
17. burn bridges - angrily act in a way that will end a relationship

Pages 44-45

Hyperboles

Directions: Use the words and phrases in the word bank to complete each of the hyperbolic statements.

1. Just looking at food makes me gain weight.

2. The coffee was so thick that a cruise ship could float on top.

3. The cat's eyes were big as saucers.

4. The window was so clean that you could see 5,000 miles away.

5. He whistled so loud that my eardrums burst.

6. Her purse was so big that a marching band came out of it when she opened it.

7. You are on my mind at least a trillion times a day.

8. The chair was so fragile that when an ant walked on it, it broke.

9. I studied so hard that my brain couldn't fit any other information into it.

10. He lies so much that the truth runs away from him.

11. Her car is so fast that she could drive around the world in one day.

12. When my father found out that I failed class, he yelled so loud that my grandmother could hear him 250 miles away.

13. The house was so filthy that the cockroaches protested and left.

14. 14. When she found out that she won the contest, her face lit up brighter than a light bulb.

15. After discovering the bug hanging above her, she jumped clear across the room.

Page 45

Similes & Metaphors

Directions: Identify each sentence as a simile or metaphor.

Simile: a comparison that uses the words like or as.

Metaphor: a comparison that does not use the words like or as.

1. The food was like a drug. simile
2. She was cool as a cucumber. simile
3. She was sharp as a pin. simile
4. Her house is an icebox. metaphor
5. The sudden downpour came down in piercing needles. metaphor
6. The sun bursting through the clouds was a ray of hope that my dreams would come true. metaphor
7. She was like a wild animal running around untamed. simile
8. His cruel words were a bullet to my bruised heart. metaphor
9. The moon beams were like a guide dog showing us the way home. simile
10. The ice cream is as hard as a brick. simile
11. The baby was a bundle of joy. metaphor
12. Life is a journey full of pleasant sights and wrong turns. metaphor
13. His feet are as long as a submarine. simile
14. She is as tall as a skyscraper. simile
15. His eyes are the color of the ocean after a storm. metaphor
16. The water is as clear as newly cleaned glass. simile
17. The turkey was lean like a ballerina. simile
18. He is as cool as ice. simile
19. She sweats like a hog. simile
20. She is as clean as a whistle. simile

Page 46

Alliterations

Alliteration is the repetition or use of the same consonant sound at the beginning of a phrase or sentence.

Example #1: Tiny Tim stood tall.

- The letter T is repeated at the beginning of more than two words in this sentence.

Example #2: She was safe and sound.

- The letter S is repeated at the beginning of more than two words in this sentence.

Directions: Read each sentence/phrase below. Identify if the sentence has an alliteration and underline all the words with the same beginning sound.

1.The food was bountiful. not an alliteration

2. **A**bby **a**te **a**n **a**pple **a**fterward. alliteration

3. **Q**uentin **q**uickly put the **q**uill **q**uietly away. alliteration

4. I went shopping downtown yesterday. not an alliteration

5. **G**oosy **G**oose alliteration

6. **S**leepy and **S**luggish alliteration

7. In the Jungle not an alliteration

8. Abby ate an apple. alliteration

9. **T**icker **T**icker **T**oc alliteration

10. Welcome Home not an alliteration

11. **M**oody **M**ax alliteration

12. She had a sweet sixteen birthday party. alliteration

13. Sullen Susan stayed still. alliteration

14. She didn't care about what other people thought. not an alliteration

15. The radio is too loud. not an alliteration

16. I really don't care what you say. not an alliteration

Page 47

Imagery

Imagery is the use of a vivid description to create pictures or images in the reader's mind.

Directions: Read the following poem and answer the following questions.

She stood out like a sore thumb,
In a dress the color of a plum.
Eyes wide with fright,
Yellow and orange streaks in hair dark as night.
All of that made her look a total sight.
Her mouth slightly open, curved to one side
Showing two oversized sharp fangs that seemed impossible to hide.
With two tiny feet, small as a snail,
A long giraffe neck and skin white and pale.
I watched her as she silently began to steal away
Being glad that it was the end of the day

1. Identify the 2 similes in the poem. with feet small as a snail; hair dark as night

2. Identify the 2 idioms in the poem. steal away; stood out like a sore thumb

Page 48

Onomatopoeia Words

Directions: Read the poem below. Underline the onomatopoeia words. Reread the poem and make the sounds instead of saying the words.

Noise! Noise! Noise!
Everywhere I go
I always hear noise!
Water splashing.
Tires squealing.
Rain trickling.
Horns honking.
Pots banging.
Bees buzzing.
Frogs croaking.
But the best noise of all
Is the pitter patter feet
Of my baby boy Skeet.

Page 49

Onomatopoeia Words

Directions: Look at each onomatopoeia word in the text box. Put each word in the correct category. Some words may fit in multiple categories.

Sounds that Animals Make	Sounds of Inanimate Objects
1. growl	1. vroom
2. hoot	2. sizzle
3. tweet	3. beep-beep
4. roar	4. crack
5. buzz	5. bang
6. bleat	6. drip
7. bray	7. twang
8. trumpet	8. whoosh
9. chirp	9. ring
10. bellow	10. snap
11. cluck	11. tick tock
12. croak	12. splash
13. oink	13. slam
14. neigh	14. ding dong
15. squeak	15. honk

Page 50

Cliché or Proverb

A cliché or proverb is a common saying that conveys a message or idea.
Example: Birds of a feather ________________.
□ drift apart □ flock together

Just from looking at the context clue "birds of a feather," you know that all the birds are similar.

Directions: Read each proverb/cliché. Select the correct answer based on the context clues provided.

1. Make it plain and simple.
2. You never know until you try. If you don't try, you can only speculate on what might have happened.
3. Absence makes the heart grow fonder.
4. Sneaky as a snake.
5. A man is known by the company he keeps. Surround yourself with people you admire and respect.
6. An apple a day keeps the doctor away.
7. Beggars can't be choosers.
8. Blood is thicker than water.
9. Curiosity killed the cat.
10. Do unto others as you want them to do unto you.

Page 51

Cliché or Proverb

Directions: Read each proverb/cliché. From reading the context clues in the sentence, select the correct answer.

1. Crime does not pay. Any gains are short-term and the consequences, if caught, are life shattering.
2. Trust me, I am not the best role model. Do as I say and not as I do.
3. Experience is the best teacher because you can learn what or what not to do.
4. A fool and his money are soon parted. Save and invest wisely.
5. Actions speak louder than words. It is often easier to say than to do.
6. Do you really want to know? I am honest, so ask me questions and I'll tell no lies.
7. Practicing correctly makes perfect.
8. A man is known by his friends. If your friends constantly lie, cheat, and steal, I will assume that you'll do the same.
9. This math problem is all wrong. You need to start from scratch.
10. Appearances can be deceiving. Looks can be deceiving, so take your time in getting to know someone.

Pages 52 - 53

Homonyms and Context Clues

Homonyms are words that are pronounced the same yet spelled differently. The words have different meanings.
Example: which and witch

Directions: Read each sentence below and select the correct answer.

1. She took her time to write the letter. She wanted to choose the right words.

2. His only role in the play was to roll down the hill.

3. Regardless of how bad the weather gets; I must decide whether to go to the party.

4. You must use the oar to row the boat, or we will remain in one spot.

5. The maid came into our room and made the bed.

6. The band was banned because of their fighting.

7. The days went by so fast that she felt as if she were in a daze.

8. For her heel to heal, she needed to keep her foot elevated.

9. He made some biscuits with the flour. Then, he went outside to pick a flower to put into the vase.

10. She began to write all her numbers, including number two, on the board. After seeing her, I wanted to write, too.

11. The vein in her forehead bulged out very far. She was very vain and angered quickly when others got attention for their appearance.

12. On Sunday, Sue went to the ice cream store to buy a sundae.

13. You need to go ahead and wrap the presents. Then, turn off that rap music!

14. The soot from the chimney turned his suit black.

15. She read her book while ironing her red dress for school.

16. Since I couldn't ride on my stationary bike, I went to get some stationery to write a letter.

17. Although he will praise you to your face, remember that he preys on small weaknesses.

18. Despite her dog's comforting paws touching her leg, she was so nervous that she had to pause before speaking.

19. She knew that some of her obligations and chores were <u>overdue</u>, but the doctor told her that she needed to take it easy and not <u>overdo</u> it.

Page 54

Homonyms

Directions: Select the correct definition.

1. wait
☐ serve ☐ <u>remain in readiness</u>

2. raze
☐ to lift up ☐ <u>to tear down completely</u>

3. seize
☐ **<u>to take</u>** ☐ to look

4. principle
☐ head of a school ☐ <u>a rule or standard</u>

5. peek
☐ <u>secret look</u> ☐ top

6. incite
☐ <u>to provoke</u> ☐ within one's view

7. too
☐ toward ☐ <u>also</u>

8. tolled
☐ spoke ☐ <u>rang</u>

9. assent
☐ <u>to agree</u> ☐ go up mountain

10. coarse
☐ path ☐ <u>rough</u>

11. tail
☐ <u>extension from an animal's behind</u> ☐ story

12. week
☐ not strong ☐ seven days

13. scent
☐ send away ☐ smell

14. steel
☐ to take away ☐ piece of metal

Pages 57 - 58

Compound Words

Directions: Look at the words below. Put an X in the box by the compound word.

1. ☐ began ☐ turnaround ☐ hopeful ☐ relations
2. ☐ already ☐ battlefield ☐ regain ☐ untapped
3. ☐ began ☐ reborn ☐ amusement ☐ paperclip
4. ☐ crackdown ☐ scanner ☐ blindly ☐ gopher
5. ☐ intercom ☐ passerby ☐ liability ☐ present
6. ☐ engineering ☐ cupful ☐ piggyback ☐ weekly
7. ☐ masterpiece ☐ supportive ☐ imagery ☐ hurriedly
8. ☐ pioneer ☐ remain ☐ pileup ☐ diverse
9. ☐ commitment ☐ layover ☐ founder ☐ retired
10. ☐ downsize ☐ owner ☐ relative ☐ believer
11. ☐ university ☐ organization ☐ twofold ☐ blindly
12. ☐ mastermind ☐ coincidence ☐ quickly ☐ progress
13. ☐ introduce ☐ stapler ☐ farfetched ☐ computerized
14. ☐ corkscrew ☐ amusement ☐ semester ☐ resemblance

15. ☐ buoy ☐ homestretch ☐ realness ☐ evolution

16. ☐ foreign ☐ disloyal ☐ drawbridge ☐ cynic

17. ☐ calculation ☐ falter ☐ expression ☐ aftermath

18. ☐ eyesore ☐ trivial ☐ renounce ☐ havoc

19. ☐ disheveled ☐ avid ☐ coastline ☐ atmosphere

20. ☐ alien ☐ dingy ☐ confide ☐ skateboard

21. ☐ worthwhile ☐ considerate ☐ strategy ☐ random

22. ☐ somber ☐ guideline ☐ fossil ☐ dissect

23. ☐ exercise ☐ tornado ☐ waterproof ☐ arrangement

24. ☐ language ☐ logical ☐ narrative ☐ shortchange

25. ☐ comprehensive ☐ proofread ☐ objective ☐ howling

26. ☐ mountainside ☐ tomorrow ☐ structure ☐ statements

27. ☐ quietly ☐ request ☐ trustworthy ☐ variety

28. ☐ yardstick ☐ advanced ☐ discussions ☐ details

29. ☐ economy ☐ popularity ☐ modify ☐ footprint

30. ☐ tallest ☐ weeklong ☐ expand ☐ shutter

31. ☐ reverses ☐ swallowing ☐ hotheaded ☐ mixture

32. ☐ preacher ☐ birdbrain ☐ detective ☐ mechanics

33. ☐ eyeballs ☐ collective ☐ equipment ☐ champion

34. ☐ handling ☐ eliminate ☐ heavyweight ☐ striving

35. ☐ ripens ☐ menace ☐ details ☐ quicksand

Page 59

Compound Words

Directions: Use words from the word bank to form compound words.

1. understood
2. awestruck
3. hopeless
4. downtrodden
5. laughingstock
6. headache
7. bookshelf
8. butterfly
9. freethinker
10. paintbrush
11. mailbox
12. crestfallen
13. cheapskate
14. tryouts
15. standstill
16. homework
17. eyelid
18. cobweb
19. citizenship
20. brainstorm

Page 60

Matching Definitions

Directions: Match the words in the word box to its definition.

1. full of defiance - hostile
2. destiny - fate
3. speak in lively way - chirpy
4. emphasized - accentuated
5. in concord; harmony - unison
6. sufficient or adequate - suffice
7. side by side - abreast
8. outside of the regular curriculum - extracurricular
9. to achieve - attain
10. not faltering or hesitating - undaunted
11. forgetful, unmindful, or unaware - oblivious
12. struggled; anguished - agonized
13. something that happens often - frequent
14. new or inexperienced - novice
15. reasonable thought - rational
16. scattered - strewed
17. insufficient amount - scarce
18. idle or passing notion - whim

Page 62

Connotations

Directions: Look at the words in each set below. Underline the word in each set with the most positive connotation.

1. lounge, lazy, goof off, bum

2. colorful, loud, bright, blinding

3. inarticulate, dumb, idiotic, stupid

4. raging, furious, angry, irate

5. agreeable, push-over, sap, doormat

6. child-like, immature, infantile, youthful

7. wail, cry, howl, squall

8. gossip, babble, talk, blab

9. crazy, unique, eccentric, unusual

10. guest, intruder, interloper, visitor

11. content, smug, egomaniac, self-centered

12. tread, squash, tramp, overwhelm

13. peculiar, eccentric, unique, quirky

14. evaporated, parched, dehydrated, shriveled

15. argue, debate, fuss, confront

16. ask, pry, delve, interrogate

17. welt, inflammation, swelling, blister

18. smart, egghead, nerd, geek

19. stimulate, instigate, wheedle, provoke

20. stubborn, defiant, resolute, hard-headed

Pages 63 - 64

Connotations

Directions: Each of the following sentences includes a pair of words with similar dictionary definitions, but different connotations. Put an X in the box with the correct connotation.

1. She was so ____________around his dog that he put the dog outside.
☐ prudish ☐ <u>squeamish</u>

2. The girl tried to ___________ out the sour candy.
☐ <u>spit</u> ☐ eject

3. Mary Ann was so ___________________ that she sat in the back of the class so that she wouldn't have to talk to anyone.
☐ <u>bashful</u> ☐ reserved

4. The dog _______________ in pain when he got his shots.
☐ <u>yelped</u> ☐ barked

5. She was so ______________ that she tripped over the stool.
☐ gawky ☐ <u>clumsy</u>

6. The ______________ of the accident demolished both cars.
☐ shock ☐ <u>impact</u>

7. You could see through the glass, for the house was __________________.
☐ unsullied ☐ <u>immaculate</u>

8. We had a diverse group of people at Billy's ___________________________.
☐ <u>party</u> ☐ high tea

9. The teen was so out of control that some people viewed him as being ______________.
☐ negligent ☐ <u>delinquent</u>

10. The employees decided to _______________ due to low wages.
☐ blockade ☐ <u>picket</u>

11. Ever since the book fell on his head, he has suffered memory ______________.
☐ reversions ☐ <u>lapses</u>

12. She was so ____________ that she thought that she was better than everyone else.
☐ conceited ☐ boastful

13. Even though the knife _______________ his lung, he survived.
☐ sliced ☐ punctured

14. The house was _______________ by the floodwaters.
☐ destroyed ☐ devoured

15. In the spring, our flowers started ______________.
☐ vegetating ☐ budding

16. Ignoring my sign, the man ________________ onto my property.
☐ invaded ☐ trespassed

17. Even though he had a job, he was called a ____________ since he hid from all work.
☐ wanderer ☐ loafer

18. He looked so ___________ that it seemed as if a slight wind could topple him.
☐ inferior ☐ puny

19. The ____________ from the bank caused considerable stress.
☐ defrauding ☐ theft

20. To ____________ him, she sent her son to his room.
☐ sentence ☐ punish

21. He looked very _________________ at his retirement ceremony.
☐ stiffed-necked ☐ dignified

Pages 65 - 66

Connotations

Directions: Read each sentence. Make a new sentence by changing the underlined connotation to a new word. Select a new word from the box below.

1. She talks constantly.

She argues constantly.

2. Her plans were unclear to me.

Her plans were disorderly to me.

3. You could see the look of despair in his eyes.

You could see the look of uncertainty in his eyes.

4. The man's actions were so lame that I felt sick.

The man's actions were so despicable that I felt sick.

5. The plans were doomed from the start because the conditions were unfavorable.

The plans were doomed from the start because the conditions were hostile.

6. She directed everyone to sit down and listen.

She pressured everyone to sit down and listen.

7. Her lies were cruel as well as vindictive.

Her lies were cruel as well as unforgiving.

8. She was always absent from school.

She was always truant from school.

9. His trick did not work, for she immediately knew that he was lying.

His deception did not work, for she immediately knew that he was lying.

10. Linda was so unpredictable that she was fired the second day.

Linda was so reckless that she was fired the second day.

11. The bump made him hit his head on the pavement.

The impact made him hit his head on the pavement.

12. He was punished by being made to sit in time-out.

He was penalized by being made to sit in time-out.

13. She was so self - seeking that it was irritating to be around her.

She was so egotistical that it was irritating to be around her.

14. Dehydration made him unable to complete the race.

Dehydration made him unfit to complete the race.

15. Losing the contest made him feel sad.

Losing the contest made him feel grief - stricken.

Page 67

Connotations

Directions: Circle the word with the most negative connotation.

1 dreamy preoccupied absent-minded

2. scent rancid smell

3. vintage antique outdated

4. bother torment tease

5. preoccupied inattentive delirious

6. youthful childish lively

7. self-confident assured vain

8. persuade argue convince

9. accidental forgetful negligent

10. gossip chat converse

Directions: Circle the word with the most positive connotation.

11. sneered smiled smirked

12. shy timid meek

13. economical cheap cut-rate

14. smug superior assured

15. stubborn determined headstrong

16. eager impatient anxious

17. squabble quarrel discussion

18. prying inquisitive nosey

19. bold cocky brash

20. interrogated questioned challenged

Page 68

Connotations

Directions: Match the words in the word box to its match. The first one is done for you.

1. yell - shriek
2. hit - whack
3. underprivileged - destitute
4. fury - wrath
5. haunt - obsess
6. frugal - thrifty
7. futile - useless
8. chastise - reprimand
9. misbehaved – ill-mannered
10. rumor - gossip
11. numb - unfeeling
12. weave - stagger
13. mock - scorn
14. recluse - homebody
15. ruthless - unsympathetic
16. stain - blemish

Page 69

Opposites

Directions: Underline the two words or phrases in each group that are opposite in meaning to the underlined vocabulary word.

1. reality realism falsity realness fiction
2. crucial important immaterial relevant irrelevant
3. succumb yield perish survive make it
4. capable unable resourceful susceptible able
5. undaunted shaken cowardly determined unshaken
6. resounding ringing quiet weakening reverberating
7. sophisticated naïve cultivated gullible educated
8. fashionable stylish frumpy faddish dowdy
9. expert proficient unskilled adept unprofessional
10. concluded ended unfinished terminated began
11. resplendent ugly glorious colorless splendid
12. oblivious unmindful mindful observant unaware
13. affirm contradict confirm negate support
14. enhanced decreased reduced increased intensified
15. defiant compliant resistant easygoing insubordinate
16. deteriorated recuperate crumble worsen recovered
17. hostile amicable unthreatening bitter belligerent
18. challenging easy difficult thought-provoking boring
19. glowing dull bright luminous unenthusiastic
20. wisdom wise sensible folly foolishness
21. lush little plush abundant scarce

Page 70

Vocabulary

Directions: Choose the correct word from the word box to complete each of the following sentences. Some of the words will not be used.

1. She desperately wanted to win the prize.
2. It was crucial that he took his medication.
3. She felt compelled to speak out against what she believed was wrong.
4. He didn't want to succumb to fatigue, so he took a small break.
5. Since he took a gamble on a whim, he lost everything.
6. They made a pact that they would be friends forever.
7. She felt disillusioned over losing the contest.
8. The impact of the harsh words caused her to fall into a depression.
9. The intensity of the flames caused the firefighters to move back.
10. He has the potential to achieve all his dreams.
11. He knew that his only chance of survival was to grab the rope.
12. Even though she was capable of making good grades, she felt pressured to act like she wasn't smart.
13. The boy was awestruck at how pretty she was.
14. The lie was so far-fetched that no one believed him.
15. She could not comprehend the magnitude of the problem.
16. Her reflection in the mirror made her smile.
17. Her goal was to win the contest.
18. She did not want to believe the reality of the situation.
19. The obstacles were so great that she felt like giving up.
20. The intricacy of the puzzle caused her to give up.
21. She refused to accept her fate because she wanted to win.
22. She agonized over her decision so much that she became tired.

Page 71

Vocabulary

Directions: Choose the correct word from the list below to complete each of the following sentences. Some of the words will not be used.

1. Since she was an expert in the subject matter, they hired her.
2. There were numerous mistakes in her homework.
3. She had a smug look on her face because she was sure that she had won.
4. It was no coincidence that he was seated at the same table as his secret admirer.
5. He looked very fashionable in his new suit.
6. Because of her exhaustion, she fainted after the race.
7. He was undaunted by the jeers of the crowd.
8. Her test results were extraordinary compared to other students.
9. The resounding noise caused her ears to ache.
10. He felt gratitude toward the judges for choosing him.
11. The criteria for winning were not clear.
12. He tried to intimidate her by blocking her path.
13. Her extracurricular activities caused her to fall behind in her grades.
14. Her growth spurt caused her to grow two inches in three months.
15. She had practically won the contest but lost in the last few seconds.

Page 72

Vocabulary

Directions: Choose the correct word from the list below to complete each of the following sentences. Some of the words will not be used.

1. She didn't know all the problems that she would encounter.

2. More emphasis was placed on talent than beauty.

3. She concluded that the main cause of the problem was Eric.

4. The dew on the grass made it glisten.

5. She was perturbed at his disruptive behavior.

6. The arguments caused everyone to become tense.

7. He sarcastically remarked that she wouldn't have won if he hadn't tripped.

8. To become a winner, you must first visualize yourself as one.

9. His admiration of the gang leader caused him to make wrong choices.

10. Even though the interior of the house looked good, the exterior was worn.

11. Her problems were so overwhelming that she cried a lot.

12. She reassured him that everything would be fine.

13. Because of his disguise, no one recognized him.

14. She was oblivious to the dangers that she faced.

15. In anticipation of the money she was to receive, she went shopping.

16. In comparison to the other job, this job pays more.

17. She was determined to attain her goals.

18. The incident happened so long ago that she vaguely remembered the details.

Page 73

Vocabulary

Directions: Choose the correct word from the list below to complete each of the following sentences. Some of the words will not be used.

1. The cheerleaders cheered in unison.
2. She did not understand the directions, so she asked him to clarify.
3. Exercising was a big challenge for her since she hated doing it.
4. She didn't want to mingle because she was shy.
5. The bees swarmed around the flowers.
6. They slowly proceeded to the finish line.
7. She had a big adjustment to make in her new job.
8. A lot of people were duped by the con man.
9. It takes a lot of discipline to exercise consistently.
10. The odds were against them from the very beginning.
11. They were all achievers, for they made the honor roll.
12. Due to the insistence of his mom, Ben hired a tutor.
13. He won primarily through cheating.
14. Winning the game looked bleak because they were behind by twenty points.
15. Since she had high test scores, the prospects of going to college looked good.
16. The storm didn't cease until five hours later.
17. Her friends were a hindrance to her.
18. Because she had lost many pounds, her weight loss was too drastic.
19. His status as class president was unchallenged.
20. Juan's popularity caused him to believe that he was better than his friends.
21. There are many possibilities in your career choice.
22. Due to her affirming statements, Betty felt that she could achieve her dreams.

Page 74

Vocabulary

Directions: Choose the correct word from the list below to complete each of the following sentences. Some of the words will not be used.

1. The wedding procession moved slowly.

2. The leaves swirled around the yard.

3. Her perspective on the situation was different from his.

4. He left his clothes strewed around the room.

5. Her mind deteriorated so quickly that it was difficult for her to remember things.

6. His friends had such a great influence on him that he couldn't make decisions on his own.

7. The grass was lush and green.

8. Even though she felt pain, she did not flinch.

9. The furniture was so old that it was considered antique.

10. The light was glowing so brightly that it made her eyes hurt.

11. The environment was so hostile that they began to feel tense.

12. The dress accentuated her figure.

13. They viewed the other team as losers.

14. Algebra was very challenging to her.

15. She felt despair because everything was going wrong.

16. The child was very defiant and determined to do it his way.

17. Her appearance made her look older than she really was.

18. Even though she was only fifteen, she had the wisdom of a much older person.

19. The mountain was vast in comparison to the smaller hills.

20. Her grades enhanced her chances of getting into a good college.

21. His chances of making the football team were vanishing before him.

22. Working two jobs became a burden because she was always tired.

Pages 75-77

Commonly Confused Words

Directions: When two words have similar sounds or spellings, it can be confusing! Write the correct word to complete each sentence.

choose chose

1. It was difficult for her to choose a gift. Finally, she chose a gift card.

lose loose

2. He did not mean to lose his belt. Now his pants are loose without his belt.

and an

3. She wanted cookies and candy. But her mom told her to eat an apple.

wonder wander

4. Even though I was told not to wander by my mom, I did so anyway. Now I wonder how to find her in the crowded store.

emigrated immigrated

5. Upon adulthood, he emigrated from the Middle East to the United States. A few years later, his parents immigrated too.

stationery stationary

6. For exercise, she rides her stationary bike in her basement. While riding her bike, she noticed that she needed more stationery paper.

coarse course

7. Sue enrolled in a sewing course. In her first class, she learned about coarse material.

effect affect

8. The loud music outside Jean's window did affect her ability to sleep. The next day, Jean's neighbor apologized for any effect his loud music had on her.

capital Capitol

9. Washington D.C. is the capital of the United States. In D.C., the U.S. Congress meet in the building named the United States Capitol.

clothes cloths

10. You need to iron your clothes. Afterwards, dust the furniture with the new cloths.

forth fourth

11. Can we please move forth to get the job done? This is the fourth time we had a delay.

brought bought

12. At the store, she bought herself a beautiful pastel dress to wear to the party. The salesperson brought it to her in a plastic bag for transport.

compliment complement

13. The tie complemented his suit. At the party, he received lots of compliments.

precede proceed

14. Because Dan did not know the right route, Lily told him to proceed to the first walkway. To see if he knew the route back, Lily told Dan that he could precede her.

lie lay

15. Please lay the book down. Afterwards, go and lie down and take a nap.

too to

16. Please go to bed. Today has been too hectic and you should be tired.

collaborate corroborate

17. To prove or disapprove the theory, we must collaborate to meet the deadline. If everything proves to be true, our focus should be to corroborate the theory with our evidence.

who whom

18. Who is going to the park with me? I am going to meet a group of friends whom I have known for many years.

fewer less

19. Because of his strict practice sessions, Reggie found that he was making fewer mistakes. However, he learned that some weeks he could do with less practice.

buy by

20. I had to go to the store to buy some fruit. I stopped by the bank to withdraw some money.

Pages 78-79

Context Clues

Readers can use context clues to figure out the meanings of unknown words. Context clues are hints used to assist readers in understanding unknown words. Context clues may be in the same sentence as the unknown words or in sentences that come before or after them.

Example: Jewel purposefully spilled her drink on Tanya. To not get in trouble, she pretended it was an accident.

You can conclude the word purposefully means planned because Jewel pretended it was an accident.

Directions: Choose the correct word to complete each of the following sentences. Use context clues to find the meaning of the underlined words.

1. Since all the evidence was inconclusive, the charges were dropped due to insufficient evidence.
☐ provable ☐ circumstantial ☐ verifiable

2. The smell penetrated the whole house. We had to open all the windows.
☐ entered ☐ exited ☐ halfway through

3. She was renowned in her community for being an excellent and popular singer.
☐ unfamiliar ☐ celebrated ☐ criticized

4. Even though we tried to shield her from his lies, she was soon exposed to them.
☐ expose ☐ safeguard ☐ uncover

5. His plans were so obscure that she urged him to make them more defined.
☐ clear ☐ plain ☐ vague

6. He was known as a liar, so she was reluctant to trust him.
☐ eager ☐ unwilling ☐ ready

7. Even though she didn't realize it, her life was in jeopardy because of the risk of falling rocks.
☐ danger ☐ valid ☐ side

8. Using her charm, she beguiled him into believing all her lies.
☐ expose ☐ misled ☐ revealed

9. Instead of rushing to decide, she took her time to ponder the situation.
☐ consider ☐ ignore ☐ disregard

10. He made such a rash decision that he felt foolish afterwards.
☐ cautionary ☐ hurried ☐ careful

11. It was such a wintry day that we stayed in to drink hot chocolate and snuggle by the fire.
☐ windy ☐ warm ☐ chilly

12. The animals ravaged the garden leaving only weeds.
☐ ruined ☐ saved ☐ protected

13. Her outfit was so striking that she received many compliments.
☐ ordinary ☐ remarkable ☐ unattractive

14. Because of his bad reputation and being known as an outcast, no one talked to him.
☐ outsider ☐ insider ☐ employee

15. She was prudent with her money because she was saving to buy a car.
☐ hasty ☐ careless ☐ careful

16. She kept knocking my books down to provoke me.
☐ aggravate ☐ avoid ☐ pacify

17. The teacher had to reprimand her for being continually late to class.
☐ compliment ☐ punish ☐ praise

18. The pain began to lessen as the medication took effect.
☐ diminish ☐ intensify ☐ magnify

Pages 80-81

Context Clues

Directions: Choose the one word or phrase that best keeps the meaning of the underlined word.

Sarah did not want to get into an altercation with Mary. Whenever she saw Mary, she went out of her way to avoid her.

1. Select the meaning of the word altercation.
☐ reconcile ☐ heated argument ☐ friendly debate

The colicky baby cried and cried. The father tried his best to pacify the baby by whatever means necessary.

2. Select the meaning of the word pacify.
☐ soothe ☐ enrage ☐ provoke

Lila knew something was wrong with Devin's insistence that they should be friends. She was finally able to discern that he was only after her money.

3. Select the meaning of the word discern.
☐ ignore ☐ overlook ☐ recognize

The lawyer knew the witness was not telling the truth. He was finally able to invalidate his claims through the testimony of one eyewitness.

4. Select the meaning of the word invalidate.
☐ support ☐ prove false ☐ prove true

Because she had an amiable personality, it was easy for her to make friends. No matter where she went, people were drawn to her.

5. Select the meaning of the word amiable.
☐ disagreeable ☐ friendly ☐ aloof

Laughing, Billy stepped on the girl's toe as he ran past her. The girl was astonished by his level of disrespect.

6. Select the meaning of the word astonished.
☐ unruffled ☐ shocked ☐ indifferent

Patricia couldn't understand why Dave was still angry. She felt that their argument was just a petty misunderstanding.

7. Select the meaning of the word petty.
☐ mammoth ☐ small ☐ enormous

Even though she was a natural athlete, her zeal to win caused her to cheat. Due to this, she was disqualified from the last race.

8. Select the meaning of the word zeal.
☐ disinterest ☐ indifference ☐ determination

Beatrice had excellent study habits. She was staunch in her beliefs that good study habits would help her earn good grades.

9. Select the meaning of the word staunch.
☐ steadfast ☐ wavering ☐ fluctuating

He hated his job. The work was too tedious. He was tired of doing the same thing over and over, day in and day out.

10. Select the meaning of the word tedious.
☐ boring ☐ exciting ☐ interesting

They denounced him because of his evil ways.

11. Select the meaning of the word denounced.
☐ applauded ☐ condemned ☐ flattered

Page 85

Spelling

Directions: Read each sentence. Write the correct spelling of the frequently misspelled underlined word. If the underlined word is spelled correctly, write "correct."

1. My dad asked me to vacum the carpet. vacuum
2. We had to manever past the cars. maneuver
3. I returned the merchandice to the store. merchandise
4. We ate at my favorite restarant. restaurant
5. They were so exhausted that they flopped on the ground. Correct
6. My competiter was sure that she would win. competitor
7. This was a special occassion. occasion
8. She wrote a weekly column for a newspaper. Correct
9. His tardiness has occured more than once. occurred
10. There's no guaratee that you will win. guarantee
11. They were usualy late. usually
12. You had to get a mininum score of 70% to pass. minimum
13. Everyone could see that the child recklessly running around the store lacked disciapline. discipline
14. Your going to get in trouble if you don't stop. You're
15. Wanting to tell a more exciting story, she decided to exagerate the situation. exaggerate
16. Due to his lack of attention, he acidentaly stumbled and fell. accidentally
17. It was so cold that all the games were cancelled. Correct
18. Do you realy want to go to the park? really
19. All the comitee members voted against the proposal. committee
20. The do on the grass made it very wet. dew

Pages 85 -88

Spelling

Directions: Put an X in the box with the correct answer. You may use the dictionary.

1. Whether you ______________ my decision or not, you must abide by it.
   ☐ except ☐ accept

2. Everyone is going ______________ Dana.
   ☐ accept ☐ except

3. Before you ______________ any further, you need to talk to Ann.
   ☐ proceed ☐ precede

4. Since she was the shortest, she ______________ him in line.
   ☐ proceeded ☐ preceded

5. The dog wagged ______ tail in anticipation.
   ☐ it's ☐ its

6. _______ so cold outside that she is trembling.
   ☐ It's ☐ Its

7. They _____________ to the country in which they were born.
   ☐ emigrated ☐ immigrated

8. They __________________ to a country they had never been.
   ☐ emigrated ☐ immigrated

9. I need to __________ down and get some rest.
   ☐ lie ☐ lay

10. Just ______ the book on the sofa.
    ☐ lie ☐ lay

11. Make sure you wear gloves because the _______________ may burn your skin.

☐ lie ☐ lye

12. _______ knocking at the door?
    ☐ Whose ☐ Who's

13. __________ toy is on the floor?
☐ Whose ☐ Who's

14. We went to the _______ where the play was to be held.
☐ cite ☐ site

15. In research papers, you must always ________ where you got your information from.
☐ cite ☐ site

16. _______ the dish down now before you drop it!
☐ Sit ☐ Set

17. You need to _______ down so that other people can see.
☐ sit ☐ set

18. The ____________ to the story is to always be prepared.
☐ morale ☐ moral

19. Her ________ was so low that she didn't try to win.
☐ morale ☐ moral

20. ________ so conniving that it is absolutely sickening.
☐ Your ☐ You're

21. You need to stop _________ yelling.
☐ your ☐ you're

22. Are you going to take my ___________?
☐ advise ☐ advice

23. I would ____________ you to think before you act.
☐ advise ☐ advice

24. He is so _________ at karate that he easily earned his black belt.
☐ good ☐ well

25. Even though he had been in the hospital for a week, he looked __________.
☐ good ☐ well

26. I am so tired that I can't run any ______________.
☐ farther ☐ further

27. Since I don't understand, I will need __________ instructions.
☐ farther ☐ further

28. Her cry ____________ people coming to her aid.
☐ illicited ☐ elicited

29. He was constantly in and out of jail for doing __________ things.
☐ illicit ☐ elicit

30. You have ______________ many clothes in your closet.
□ too □ to

31. You have _____ stop with the negativity.
□ to □ too

Pages 88 - 89

Spelling Errors

Directions: Identify the spelling error in each sentence. Underline the error and write the correct spelling of the word. The first one is done for you.

1. She befriended the girls because she really wanted to be populor. popular

2. I want some pie, to. too

3. Even though I asked him not to, he decided to move fourth with the project. forth

4. Sue sold many items at the annaul bazaar. annual

5. Brue had all ready gone by the time we made it there. already

6. Climbing the ladder to paint the sealing, he saw the windows also needed cleaning. ceiling

7. When I moved to a new school, the first person I met was the principle. principal

8. The pudding is in the dairy isle. aisle

9. Although she wanted to inspire change, she did not want to insight violence. incite

10. The flower was reel, not artificial. real

11. Putting fertilizer on the grass had a positive affect. effect

13. The artist painted a beautiful seen of the beach. scene

15. The material was so course that it hurt my skin. coarse

16. He included a acknowledgement in his speech. an

17. Please chose between all the items. choose

18. Could you please go buy the store before coming home? by

19. I was hopeing for a more positive outcome. hoping

20. The knife was accidentaly left on the table. accidentally

21. Winning the prize was a great acheivement. achievement

22. We were early so we saw the begining. beginning
23. Are you comeing to the party early? coming

24. The ship finaly docked. finally

25. We completed our grammer worksheets. grammar

26. Our journey was finaly coming to an end. finally

27. The comittee members finally decided. committee

28. The goverment came to a halt. government

29. Could you vacum the floor? vacuum

30. Did you schedale your appointment? schedule

Page 90

Single Consonant

The consonants are B, C, D, F, G, H, J, K, L, M, N, P, Q, R, S, T, V, W, X, Z, and sometimes Y.

Directions: Complete each word below with a single consonant.

1. popcorn
2. x-ray
3. biography
4. multiply
5. queen
6. patient
7. scissors
8. height
9. courage
10. kitchen
11. quiz
12. demonstrate
13. zigzag
14. headache
15. garbage
16. community
17. requirement
18. frighten
19. people
20. vocabulary

Page 91

Double Consonant

Directions: Each word in the left column is misspelled. All are missing a consonant. Correctly spell each word. The first one is done for you.

Incorrectly Spelled Word	Doubled Consonant	Correctly Spelled Word
piza	z	pizza
accomodate	m	accommodate
spagheti	t	spaghetti
dismis	s	dismiss
compeled	l	compelled
glosary	s	glossary
shutle	t	shuttle
hapy	p	happy
mispell	s	misspell
blizard	z	blizzard
cabage	b	cabbage
adition	d	addition
folow	l	follow
pupet	p	puppet
peny	n	penny
aggresive	s	aggressive
hury	r	hurry
plumet	m	plummet
ballon	o	balloon
colect	l	collect
presure	s	pressure
mudy	d	muddy
scisors	s	scissors
arive	r	arrive
ofice	f	office

Page 92

Consonant Digraph

A consonant digraph is a sequence of two or more different letters which represents a single sound.

Directions: Complete each word below with a consonant digraph from the box below.

ch wr sh gh kn wh ph th

1. quench
2. thing
3. graph
4. change
5. whim
6. thought
7. chaplain
8. ghastly
9. smooth
10. orphan
11. wreck
12. rewash
13. knot
14. therapist
15. photographic
16. chase
17. flash

Page 93

Consonant Digraph

Directions: Complete each word below with a consonant digraph from the box below.

wh th ph ch wr sh ng gh kn wh ph

1. doing
2. wharf
3. spring
4. squash
5. thing
6. knead
7. long
8. gopher
9. scratch
10. chorus
11. theory
12. ash
13. sting
14. knotty
15. bough
16. whimper
17. phony
18. shrub

Page 94

Consonant Blends

Consonant blends occur when two consonants run into one another or blend and both letters are heard. (Examples: nt, sp, or br)

Directions: Complete each word below with a consonant blend from the box below.

bl br cl cr dr fl fr gl gr ll pl pr sn st sp sc

1. drowsy
2. clumsy
3. hull
4. dream
5. plural
6. plan
7. clothes
8. special
9. grasp
10. frantic
11. brazen
12. gasp
13. grade
14. scratch
15. draw
16. frenzy
17. blanket
18. flash
19. sport

Page 95

Consonant Blends

Directions: Write "yes" on the blank line to the word that has a consonant blend and "no" if the word doesn't. Underline the consonant blend.

1. threaten yes
2. eraser no
3. holiday no
4. shelf yes
5. against yes
6. paper no
7. breeze yes
8. hip no
9. imagery no
10. scream yes
11. pigeon no
12. against yes
13. penguin yes
14. pop no
15. creature yes
16. power no
17. scurry yes
18. green yes
19. complete yes
20. lamp yes

Page 96

Contractions

A contraction is a single word made up of two combined words. You create a contraction by leaving out one or more letters and using an apostrophe in place of the missing letters.

Example: After school, they will go to the park.
Revised with a contraction: After school, they'll go to the park.

1. they are they're
2. of the clock o'clock
3. you have you've
4. is not isn't
5. do not don't
6. they would they'd
7. should not shouldn't
8. I had I'd
9. cannot can't
10. we would we'd
11. it is it's
12. were not weren't
13. he would he'd
14. I have I've
15. will not won't

Page 97

Contractions

Directions: There are two words in each sentence that can be combined to make a contraction. Underline the words and write the new contraction.

Example: Who is responsible for putting the drinks on the table? Who's

1. She felt sick because she had eaten too much food to eat. she'd

2. He was too dizzy to stand and could not attend class. couldn't

3. Who will go first? Who'll

4. KJ must not be late again for practice. mustn't

5. They will first have to apologize before coming inside. they'll

6. Before taking the test, you will need to study. you'll

7. It is so cold outside that they brought the animals inside. It's

8. He had exhausted all options. He'd

9. Before leaving, they had eaten breakfast. they'd

10. At the very least, you have got to try. You've

11. Because the flowers wilted, I will need to buy more. I'll

12. They would first have to go to the store. They 'd

13. Gina ran very fast, but she could not catch up to Pat. couldn't

14. We have ten more days before my birthday party. We've

15. Even though you want to go first, let us wait. let's

16. Even though I started early, I would need to stay late. I'd

17. Stop now before you are in trouble. you're

Pages 98-99

Common Words

Directions: Four of the five words in each group have something in common. Underline the word in each group that doesn't belong. Use the word bank to write what they have in common on the line.

Example: tropical polar beach temperate dry Examples of climate types

1. fantasy science fiction mystery puppetry biography
   Examples of book genres

2. spiders butterflies grasshoppers ladybugs moths
   Examples of insects

3. Artic Lake Huron Indian Pacific Atlantic
   Names of oceans

4. Violet Daffodil Elm Lily Iris
   Names of flowers

5. propellor stern cockpit wings rudder
   Parts of Airplane

6. monitor mouse paper keyboard Internet
   Names of computer components

7. zoo rainforest forest grasslands mountains
   Examples of natural animal habitats

8. bumpy moist organ smooth skeleton
   Describes a tongue

9. earthquakes rain dust storms floods tornadoes
   Examples of environmental disasters

10. pupil taste buds cornea retina lashes
    Parts of eyes

11. chicken nuggets milkshakes buffet hamburgers curly fries
    Examples of fast food

12. pear apple pomegranate mushroom raspberry
Types of fruits

13. mole locust beaver chipmunk rat
Names of animals/insects that live underground

14. planets stars comets ocean galaxy
Describe space

15. word search jigsaw landscape crossword sudoku
Kinds of puzzles

16. aurora star heat plankton solar system
Describes sun

17. molars opinions quadrants chew thirty-two
Describes teeth

18. soccer baseball tennis summarize football
Examples of sports

19. latitude/longitude lines legend or key scale watch compass rose
Parts of a map

20. eaglet peachick lamb gosling gorilla
Names of baby animals

21. Wyoming Oregon Richmond Arkansas Vermont
Names of states

22. Guitar Electric Clarinet Saxophone Tambourine
Names of musical instruments

23. Charles R. Drew, M.D. Anna Connelly Mickey Mouse Thomas Edison
George Washington Carver
Names of inventors

24. Running Person Thing Place Idea
Examples of nouns

Made in the USA
Columbia, SC
22 June 2025

59721656R00093